THREE LECTURES
ON THE
SCIENCE OF LANGUAGE
AND ITS
PLACE IN GENERAL EDUCATION

THREE LECTURES
ON THE
SCIENCE OF LANGUAGE
AND ITS
PLACE IN GENERAL EDUCATION

DELIVERED AT THE

OXFORD UNIVERSITY EXTENSION MEETING

1889

With a Supplement "My Predecessors," an Essay on the Genesis of the Idea of the Identity of Thought and Language in the History of Philosophy.

BY

F. MAX MULLER

FIRST LECTURE:	**Difference between Man and Animal.**
	No Mystery in Language.
SECOND LECTURE:	**Analysis of Language.**
	The Lesson of the Science of Language.
THIRD LECTURE:	**Thought thicker than Blood.**
	The Cradle of the Aryas.
	The Importance of Sanskrit.

GYAN

Published by

GYAN

Gyan Publishing House
5, Ansari Road
Daryaganj, New Delhi-110002
Phone: 011-47034999, 9811692060
E-mail: books@gyanbooks.com

Distribution Network
gyanbooks.com
India, USA, Canada, UK, Australia, France

ISBN : 978-81-212-2371-3 (PB)
First Published, 1889

2nd Impression 2021

Printed at: Gyan Press, Delhi.

Three Lectures on the Science of Language
and its
Place in General Education
Author: F. Max Muller

THREE LECTURES

ON THE

SCIENCE OF LANGUAGE

DELIVERED AT THE

OXFORD UNIVERSITY EXTENSION MEETING

WITH A SUPPLEMENT

MY PREDECESSORS

BY

F. MAX MÜLLER

SECOND EDITION

CHICAGO
THE OPEN COURT PUBLISHING COMPANY
1895

I have given to the Open Court Publishing Company the right of publishing my 'Three Lectures on Language' in America, and I have revised them carefully for that purpose

26 Jan. 90. F. Max Müller

TABLE OF CONTENTS.

FIRST LECTURE.

MAN AND ANIMAL.

THERE seems to be some truth after all in the old English saying that familiarity breeds contempt, or, at all events, indifference.

There is nothing we are more familiar with than our own language. We learn it, we hardly know how. While reading, writing, arithmetic, and all the rest, are not acquired without considerable effort, and are often forgotten again in later life, we learn our most difficult lesson, namely, speaking, without any conscious effort, and, however old we may grow, we never forget it again.

But I ask you, Have you ever tried to find out what this language of ours really is; how it came to us; when and where it was made; and what it was made of?

Of course, you will all say, we learnt our language from our father and mother or rather from our mother and father. Yes, but from whom did they learn it? From their parents, and these parents again from their parents, and thus *ad infinitum*.

Even this simple answer, which is by no means quite correct, is full of import, and ought to have been taken to heart far more seriously than it seems to have been by certain philosophers who maintain that parrots and other animals also learn to speak, exactly as children learn to speak, and that therefore language is after all nothing so very wonderful, and cannot be said to form an impassable barrier between man and beast. It is quite true that children now-a-days do neither create their own language nor inherit it. Speaking any given language is not an acquired habit that descends from father to son. The necessary conditions of speech, however, exist in man and in man only; for if these necessary conditions were present in the parrot as well as in man, it would indeed be strange, to say no more, that there should never have been a *Parrotese* language, and that no parrot should ever have learnt his language from his parents, and they from theirs, and thus *ad infinitum*. A parrot never learns to speak, as little as a child would ever learn to fly. These facts are so simple and so obvious that it is difficult to understand, how they can ever have been disregarded by philosophers. And yet to the present day, most thoughtful writers go on repeating the old fallacy, that a parrot learns to say "poor Polly," just as a child learns to say "poor Polly."

To put it on the lowest ground, do these philosophers not see that every child of man is the descendant of an animal that *could* frame language, and *has* framed language; while every parrot, and every other animal is the descendant of an animal that never framed a language of its own? When a parrot learns to speak, it is simply tempted to utter certain sounds, in more or less close imitation of English or French, by such rewards as sugar and other sweetmeats, or by severe punishments on the part of its keepers. As to any parrot inventing a language of its own, and teaching that language to its young, not even Mr. Romanes would believe in such a miracle.

It is therefore not enough to say that we learn our language from our parents, and they from their parents, and thus *ad infinitum.* That would be a very lazy way of handling our problem. This retrogression *ad infinitum* would be a mere confession of ignorance, and such a confession, though it is very honorable when we know that we cannot know, cannot be tolerated except in cases where we know also *why* we cannot know.

When we see the history, or, as it is now the fashion to call it, the evolution of language, we cannot help admitting that there must have been some kind of beginning. A language, such as English, for instance, does not tumble down from the sky; and, even if it did, it would have to be picked up, and to pick up a language, as you know, is not a very easy task, particularly for a person supposed to be dumb and without any idea of what language is meant for. In former times, as it seemed to be impossible to account for language as a piece of human workmanship, it was readily admitted that it was of divine workmanship, that it really had tumbled down from the sky in some way or other, and that, curiously enough, man alone of all animals then living upon earth had been able to pick it up.

But when languages began to be more carefully examined, traces of human workmanship became more and more visible, and at last the question could no longer be pushed aside, how language was made, and why man alone of all living beings should have come into possession of it.

Now I ask, If language is that which, as a matter

of fact, distinguishes man from all other animals, is it not disgraceful that we should be so careless as not to attempt to find out what language is, and why we, and we alone of all animals, enjoy the privilege of speech? I know quite well that attempts have been made again and again to show that language is not the distinguishing characteristic of man, and that animals also, though they have never yet spoken, possess the faculty of speech, and may in time begin to speak. Even Kant seems to have indulged in the hope that the chimpanzee might some day begin to speak. But if faculty means originally facility, or that which enables us to do a thing, surely it is not too much to ask, why hitherto no animal should ever have cultivated that gift; why no animal should ever have said, "I am an animal," or, "I am an ape." Mr. Romanes, in his recent work on *Mental Evolution in Man*, has done his very best to throw a bridge over the gulf that separates all animals from man, namely, language; and if *he* has failed in showing how human language could have arisen from animal utterances, I doubt whether anybody else will ever lead that forlorn hope again.

It is easy enough to show that animals communicate; but this is a fact which has never been doubted. Dogs who growl and bark leave no doubt in the mind of other dogs, or cats, or even of man, of what they mean. But growling and barking are not language, nor do they even contain the elements of language. All names are concepts, and to say that we think in concepts is only another way of saying that we think in class-names. Mr. Romanes admits this fully; in fact, the very words I have used are his own words (*loc. cit.*, p. 22, note). But has he been able to discover any traces or germs of language, or what he calls "intellectual symbolism," in any animal known to us, and more particularly in that animal from which he thinks we are more immediately descended? Evidently not. "Anthropoid apes," he says (p. 364), "are the most intelligent, and, therefore, if specially trained, would probably display greater aptitude in the matter of sign-making than is to be met with in any other kind of brute." "But," he continues, "I do not press this point. What I now refer to is the fact, that the existing species of anthropoid apes are very few in number, and appear to be all on the high road to extinction. Moreover, it is certain that none of these existing species can have been the progenitor of man, and, lastly, it is equally certain that the extinct species (or genus) which did give origin to man must have differed in several important respects from any of its existing allies. In the first place, it must have been more social in habits; and, in the next place, it was probably more vociferous than the orang, the gorilla, or the chimpanzee."

Against such arguments it seems to me that even the gods would fight in vain. We are told, that man is descended from some kind of anthropoid ape. We answer that all anthropoid apes, known to us, are neither social nor vociferous. And we are told that in that case man must be derived from an extinct ape who differed from all known apes, and was both social and vociferous. Surely, if this is a scientific argument, scientific arguments would in future rank very low indeed.

I know of no book which has proved more clearly that language forms an impassable barrier between man and beast than the book lately published by Mr. Romanes on the *Origin of Human Faculty*, though his object was the very opposite. Taking that point therefore for granted, it seems to me disgraceful that in our general system of education, and even of elementary education, no place should have been found as yet for the Science of Language, and that a single child should be allowed to grow up, without knowing the worth and value of his most precious inheritance, without knowing what language is; language, which alone distinguishes him from all other animals; language, which alone makes man man; language, which has made him the lord of nature, and has restored to him the consciousness of his own true Self.

And here I must guard at once against an outcry that is sure to be raised. It will be said that all these arguments are inspired by an ill-disguised pride, and arise from a wish to claim a higher position for man than for other animals. We are told that we ought to be more humble, and love our neighbors and venerate our ancestors, even though they were hairy apes. I plead "Not guilty" to all such charges. By suggesting motives, any discussion may be poisoned, but such suggestions have really nothing whatever to do with the question which we are discussing. If it could be proved by irrefragable evidence that only a hundred years back all our ancestors were hairy and speechless, that would not make the slightest difference in our argument. On the contrary, it would only enhance our admiration of language, which, whether in one or in a hundred centuries, could have wrought such a marvellous charge. It would only make it more incumbent on us to find out what language really is, that it should have produced, not only a new species of animal, the *homo sapiens*, but an entirely new world. That language *has* raised man into an entirely new atmosphere, an intellectual atmosphere which no other animal is able to breathe, is admitted on all sides.

Is it not disgraceful, then, I ask once more—is it not disgraceful that we should pass through life without attempting to know what that atmosphere really is from which we draw our best intellectual life? No one is considered educated without a knowledge of writing, reading, and arithmetic. To me it seems that no one should call himself educated who does not know what language is, and how it came to be what it is.

At first sight all we seem to be able to say of language is that it is wonderful, that it passes all understanding, or, as some people would say, that it is something supernatural and miraculous. That certain vibrations of air which we produce by various emissions of our breath should represent to us and to others all that has ever passed through our mind, all we have ever seen or heard or felt, all that passes before us in the countless works of nature, and all that passes within us in our own endless feelings, our imaginings, and our thoughts, is marvellous indeed. In fact, next to the great miracle of existence, there is no greater miracle than this translation of all existence into human speech and human thought.

But, as with all true miracles, so with this, our first duty is to try to interpret it, because then only will it reveal to us all that it was meant to reveal. And with regard to the miracle wrought by language, nothing is really more miraculous than its simplicity. It is generally supposed that the philosophy of language is a subject far beyond the reach of ordinary minds. I should be sorry to suppose that there were any minds which could not take in the simple lessons of the Science of Language. We never know anything truly, unless we can make it as clear as daylight to the commonest understanding. Every one of us starts from the level of the ordinary understanding, and however far he may advance, unless he has lost the thread of his own knowledge, that is, unless he has allowed his own mind to get ravelled, tangled, and knotted, he ought to be able to lead others step by step to the same eminence which he has reached himself.

In no science is this more easy than in the Science of Language. It is difficult to teach a man music who cannot play a single instrument. But we all play at least one language, and can test the teachings of the Science of Language by a reference to our own language.

I shall try therefore to show you what the Science of Language has achieved, by taking my illustrations chiefly from a language which you all know—from English. And though I cannot in a few lectures attempt to give you more than the A B C of our science, still even that A B C may be useful, and may possibly encourage some of you to pay more attention to the study of so familiar, and yet so little explored a subject as our language is. It has indeed many lessons to teach us, many mysteries to reveal to us, and there is in it more work to do for any one who wishes to do useful work, than in any other science which I know of.

When we are told that the English language consists of about 250,000 words, we are no doubt staggered, and do not know how such a number of signs could have arisen, and how they can all be kept in our memory, each in its own place. But this large number of words is really an accumulation of many centuries, and nothing like that number could have been kept alive, except through the influence of literature.

Now literature, or, at least, a written literature, is a mere accident. Let us try, therefore, to realise what a language would be which possesses as yet no literature, and, therefore, no literary standard. Such languages still exist, and we find them generally full of dialectic variety. They vary as spoken colloquially in each family; they vary still more as spoken in different clans and colonies. In both these forms, as colloquial and as dialectic, they are full of what we may call slang,—expressions started by the whims of individuals, but often retained, and admitted after a time into more general use.

The first beginning of a settled form of speech is made at public gatherings, where a language must be used that is intelligible to persons belonging to different families and coming from distant settlements. This public language, which is soon adopted for sacred poetry also, for popular legends, and for legal enactments, becomes in time what is called the sacred, the literary, or the classical dialect. But it does not absorb the whole life of a language. On the contrary, each language runs on in its natural channels of colloquial speech and dialect and slang, and supplies from time to time new material to the classical dialect.

What thus takes place before our very eyes in illiterate languages, must have taken place in all languages, and we can see the same forces at work, even now, in such highly cultivated literary forms of speech as English.

There is one kind of English which is spoken in parliament, in the pulpit, and in the courts of law, which may be called the *public*, the *ordinary*, and *recognised* English.

The *colloquial* English, as used by educated people, differs but slightly from this parliamentary English, though it admits greater freedom of construction, and a more familiar phraseology.

The *literary* English again requires still greater grammatical accuracy, and admits a number of uncommon, poetical, and even antiquated expressions which would sound strange in ordinary conversation.

The *dialectic* English is by no means extinct. The peasants in every part of England and Scotland and Ireland, though they understand a sermon in church, and read their newspaper, both of which are written in literary English, continue to speak their own language among themselves,—a language full of ancient and curious expressions which often throw much light on the history of classical English. These dialects have of late been most carefully collected, and this is a branch of study in which everybody, if only he has a well-trained ear, is able to render most valuable assistance.

Lastly, in discussing special subjects, we are driven to use a large number of *technical, scientific, foreign*, and even *slang* expressions, many of which are quite unintelligible to the ordinary speaker.

It is these technical, scientific, foreign, and slang terms which swell our dictionaries to such an enormous size. We are told that the new Oxford Dictionary will contain a quarter of a million of words. Does any one of us know 250,000 English words? I doubt it. It is extraordinary how many words this small brain of ours will hold, but there are limits to everything. In China a young man receives his first or second class in examination, according to the number of words he can read and write. But in order to obtain the place of an imperial historian, a candidate is not required to know more than 9,000. *We* do more than this. Most of us can read Shakespeare's plays, and in order to do that, we must know about 15,000 words. But though we understand most of these words (there are only about 500 to 600 words in Shakespeare which may justly be called obsolete), there are many we should never think of using ourselves. Most of us, I believe, never use more than 3,000 or 4,000 words, and we are assured that there are peasants who never use more than 300 or 400. This does not mean that they would not understand more than that number, for the Bible which they hear in church contains about 6,000 words;[1] these they would understand more or less accurately, though they would never think of using them.

NO MYSTERY IN LANGUAGE.

A language, therefore, is after all not so bewildering a thing as it seems to be, when we hear of a dictionary of 250,000 words. In fact, for all the ordinary purposes of life a dictionary of 4,000 words would be quite sufficient.

Skeat's *Etymological Dictionary of the English Language*, which confines itself to primary words,—that is to say, which would explain *luck*, but not *lucky*, *unlucky*, *luckless*,—deals with no more than 13,500 entries. Of these only 4,000 are of Teutonic origin; 5,000

[1] According to W. T. Adey, *The English of King James's Version*, the Old and New Testaments contain 6,000 words.

are taken from French; 2,700 direct from Latin, 400 from Greek, about 250 from Celtic, and the rest from various sources. If, therefore, we confine our attention to that portion of English which is Teutonic, we find that English proper consists of about 4,000 independent words, and that all the rest are derived from these.

Let us now examine some of the words which swell our dictionaries to such an enormous extent, in order to see whether they really belong to the living language, and whether we ourselves should be able to understand them.

And first of all a few *antiquated* words—words which were used some centuries ago, but are now to be found in the dictionary only.

Do you understand *anred* and *anredness*? *Anred* means single-minded. It is derived from *red* (*ræd*), purpose, plan, scheme, and, like *anfald*, German *einfältig*, meant originally not-planning, not-scheming. Hence *anredness* came to mean singleness, and in the thirteenth century people spoke of the *onrednesse of luve and onnesse of heorte.*

You might guess the meaning of *avenant* when you read in Caxton's *Myrr.*, I. xiv. 45, "*A lytil man is ofte wel made and avenaunt,*" i. e. a little man is often well-made and becoming or comely. *Avenant* is derived from *avenir*, to come, to become, and meant agreeable, becoming, handsome; but no one would use that word now.

If you saw two men fighting, and one of them were called a regular *bangster*, you might probably guess what was meant; but, though Walter Scott still uses the word in *The Abbot*, it is no longer a living word. There was an old legal expression to commit a burglary "*by bangstrie and force.*" This again would hardly be intelligible, except to the historical student of law.

There are other words which survive, but the original meaning of which has become antiquated. In the legal phrase, "by assault and battery," for instance, *battery* still retains its original meaning, namely, beating or striking. But we could no longer say, to give a boy a battery; we must say a flogging. In ordinary parlance battery now only means a number of artillery, while men of science speak also of an electric battery.

It is curious to observe in how many words the meaning deteriorates, while it very seldom improves.

A *knave* was originally a young man, in German *ein Knabe*. In the Court cards the knave is simply the page or the knight, but by no means the villain. *Villain* itself was originally simply the inhabitant of a village. A pleader once made good use of his etymological knowledge. For this is what Swift relates: "I remember, at a trial in Kent, where Sir George Rook was indicted for calling a gentleman knave and villain, the lawyer for the defendent brought off his client by alleging the words were not injurious, for *knave*, in the old and true signification, imported only a servant; and *villain* in Latin is *villicus*, which is no more than a man employed in country labor, or rather a baily."

I doubt whether in these days any Judge, if possessed of some philological knowledge, would allow such a quibble to pass, or whether in return he would not ask leave to call the lawyer an *idiot*, for *idiot*, as you know, meant originally no more than a private person, a man who does not take part in public affairs; and afterwards only came to mean an outsider, an ill-informed man, and lastly an idiot.

A *pagan* was originally, like *villain*, the inhabitant of a *pagus*, a countryman. It came to mean *heathen*, because it was chiefly in the country, outside the town, that the worshippers of the old national gods were allowed to continue. A heathen was originally a person living on the heath. Heathen, however, is not yet a term of reproach; it simply expresses a difference of opinion between ourselves and others. But we have the same word under another disguise, namely as *hoiden*. At present *hoiden* is used in the sense of a vulgar, romping girl. But in old authors it is chiefly applied to men, to clowns or louts. We may call Socrates a heathen, but we could not call him a hoiden, though we might possibly apply that name to his wife Xanthippe.

Sometimes it happens that the same word can be used both in a good and in a bad sense. *Simplicity* with us has generally a good meaning. We read in the Bible of *simplicity and godly sincerity*. But, in the same Bible the simple ones are reproved: "How long, ye simple ones, will ye love simplicity? and the scorners delight in their scorning, and fools hate knowledge?" (*Prov.* I. 22.)

If at present we were to call a boy an *imp*, he would possibly be offended. But in Spenser's time *imp* had still a very good sound, and he allows a noble lady, a lady gent, as he calls her, to address Arthur, as "Thou worthy imp" (*Faerie Queen*, I. 9. 6). Nor is there any harm in that word, for *imp* meant originally graft, and then offspring. To graft in German is *impfen*, and this is really a corruption of the Greek ἐμφύειν to implant.

Brat is now an offensive term, even when applied to a child. It is said to be a Welsh word, and to signify a rag. It may be so, but in that case it would be difficult to account for *brat* having been used originally in a good sense. This must have been so, for we find in ancient sacred poetry such expressions as, "O Abraham's brats, o broode of blessed seede."

To use the same word in such opposite meanings is possible only where there is an historical literature which keeps alive the modern as well as the antiquated usages of a language. In illiterate languages, antiquated words are forgotten and vanish.

Think of all the meanings imbedded in the word *nice!* How did they come there? The word has a long history, and has had many ups and downs in its passage through the world. It was originally the Latin *nescius*, ignorant, and it retained that meaning in old French, and likewise in old English. Robert of Gloucester (p. 106, last line) still uses the word in that sense. "He was nyce," he says, "and kowthe no wisdom," that is, he was ignorant and knew no wisdom. But if there is an ignorance that is bliss, there is also an ignorance, or unconsciousness, or simplicity that is charming. Hence an unassuming, ingenuous, artless person was likewise called nice. However, even that artlessness might after a time become artful, or, at all events, be mistaken by others for artfulness. The over-nice person might then seem fastidious, difficult to please, too dainty, and he or she was then said to be too nice in his or her tastes.

We have traced the principal meanings of *nice* from ignorant to fastidious, as applied to persons. If nice is applied to things, it has most commonly the meaning of charming; but as we speak of a fastidious and difficult person, we can also speak of a difficult matter as a nice matter, or a nice point.

At last there remained *nice*, which simply expresses general approval. Everything, in our days, is nice, not to say, awfully nice. But unless we possessed a literature in which to study the history of words, it would be simply impossible to discover why nice should express approval as well as disapproval, nay, why it should in the end become a mere emphatic expression, as when we say, "That is a nice business," or "that is a nice mess."

And here we approach a new class of words which swell our dictionaries very considerably, namely, *slang-words*. Slang is more than a colloquial and familiar expression, it always conveys the idea of being a little vulgar. It is quite true that some expressions which we call slang were perfectly correct some centuries ago, and that they have the right to claim a place among antiquated words. The Americans are very clever at making out that most of their slang was pure classical English some centuries ago. That may be so; in many cases it no doubt is so. But that does not take away the peculiar twang of what has now become slang. A distinguished American politician declared that under certain circumstances he would let the Constitution "slide." That certainly was slang. But when he was blamed for his undignified expression, he appealed to Chaucer and Shakespeare, who use the same word in such phrases as, "Wel neigh all other cures let he slyde"; she "lete her sorwe slide"; "he lets the world slide."

It is often difficult to say why certain colloquial expressions are vulgar, while others are allowed to pass. Much depends on the speaker, for you may say almost anything in English, if you know how to say it. There is no harm in saying "You bet"; yet in America it is a sign of vulgarity. "I am very dry" is slang, "I am very thirsty" is quite correct; yet thirsty meant originally dry, and we may still speak of "thirsty land," instead of dry land. *Thirsty* is connected with Latin *torrere*, to parch, Greek *τέρσεσθαι*, to become dry.

"I have been enjoying poor health" is certainly wrong, but I doubt whether poor or bad health is a solecism. It is true that health by itself means soundness of body, and is connected with *hale*, *healing*, and *whole* (for *hole*). But as we can speak of good and bad luck, there is no serious objection to our speaking of good, or bad, or indifferent health.

The frequent use of the verb *to get* is in bad taste, but again, it can hardly be called wrong. When we read, "I *got* my things packed, and *got* to the train in time, and *got* to Paris, and *got* to the hotel, and *got* my supper, and *got* sleepy, and soon *got* to bed, and *got* a good night's rest," we can understand all that is meant, but we feel offended by the poverty and vulgarity of the expression.

Sometimes, however, slang becomes utterly unintelligible, and requires a commentary except to the initiated. I shall read a sentence from a Melbourne paper, which I hope few here present will understand without the help of explanatory notes:

"Say, mate, some our'n cockneys chummed with 'em Melbourne larrikins 'at yon booze-ken. Flash coves, blacklegs, and welchers that they be, they lushed like old 'Arry till on 'em kicked the bucket. They told a bobby that coomed by as they was gents. 'That's all my heye and Betty Martin,' says he—and he slips on the darbies and brought 'em to quod."

This, no doubt, is very vulgar English, but it is English for all that, and if there ever should be a violent social revolution at Melbourne, and the lower classes should become the upper classes, it is quite possible that this kind of English might be spoken there in parliament and even in the pulpit. We must not forget that in its origin every language may be called vulgar. It is the language of the *vulgus*, before it becomes the language of literature. Even Dante calls his Italian *il volgare*, and he was the first to use that common spoken idiom for the highest literary purposes.

There are slang-dictionaries, as large as the dictionaries of any language, and I am sorry to say that even our Universities contribute every year a fair share toward new and enlarged editions of these books. *Little go*, *Moderations*, *Greats*, *to be ploughed*, *to be gulphed*, are well-known specimens of this mysterious language. There are many more which it is perhaps wiser not to mention.

As to technical and scientific terms, they are endless. Try to speak with a boot-maker or a carpenter about his own tools and his own work, and you will be surprised at the unknown treasures of the English language. Not long ago a wine-merchant to whom I had complained about some bottles of wine not being quite full, wrote to me to return the *ullaged* bottles. I did not understand *ullaged*, and I had to consult a dictionary. There I found that *eullage* in ancient French meant that which is required to fill a bottle, from *euiller*, to fill. This *euiller* is supposed to stand for *olier*, to oil. But why to oil? Because in the South of France and Italy to the present day oil is poured into a bottle, instead of corking it. That oil has to be dashed out before the wine is drunk, and a certain amount of wine is lost in that process. That is the *eullage*, and hence the *ullaged* bottle. I doubt whether my wine-merchant knew this, and it is strange that a custom which obtained only in the South of Europe of using oil for closing bottles of wine, should have produced an expression which was used in the North of Europe, where oil was never used for that purpose. That shows how words travel forward and backward over the whole world.

When I was in Cornwall I heard the smoked pilchards called by the people *Fair Maids*. I tried to find out why, and this was the result of my inquiries. These smoked pilchards are largely exported to Genua, and are eaten there during Lent. They are called in Italian *fumada*, smoked fish. The Cornish sailors picked up that word, naturalised it, gave it an intelligible meaning, and thus became, according to their own confession, exporters of fair maids. You see the Odyssey and the adventures of Ulysses are nothing compared with the adventures of our words.

A carpenter once told me that the boards of a box ought to be properly *dowald*. I did not understand what he meant, and it was only when he showed me the actual process that I saw that to *dowal* meant to *dove-tail*, to cut the ends so that they should fit like dove-tails.

Scientific terms are likewise technical terms, only put into Greek or Latin. What can be achieved in the manufacture of such terms may be gathered from the following extract from a book on Botany:[1]

"Begoniaceae, by their anthero-connectival fabric indicate a close relationship with anonaceo-hydro-

[1] Marsh, *Lectures on the English Language*, p. 186.

charideo-nymphaeoid forms, an affinity confirmed by the serpentarioid flexuoso-nodulous stem, the liriodendroid stipules, and cissoid and victorioid foliage of a certain Begonia; and if considered hypogynous, would in their triquetrous capsule, alate seed, apetalism, and tufted stamination, represent the floral fabric of Nepenthes, itself of aristolochioid affinity, while by its pitchered leaves, directly belonging to Sarracenias and Dionaeas."

I doubt whether any Englishman, unless he be a botanist by profession, would understand the hidden meaning of these sentences, and though these words have to be admitted into an English dictionary that professes to be complete, they cannot be said to form part of the commonwealth of English undefiled.

If, then, we confine our attention to those words which form the real stock in trade of the English language, our task will become much more manageable. Instead of 250,000, we shall have to deal with about 4,000 truly English words, or, if we include all French, Latin, Greek, and Celtic primaries, with 12,350 words, and then ask ourselves once more the question, Whence do they come?

No one can help seeing that even amongst the most ordinary words in English there are some which are very much alike in sound. If these words have also some similarity in meaning, we are justified in supposing that they *may* have a common origin.

Take, for instance, such words as *to bear*, *burden*, *bier*, and *barrow*. They all have the same constituent element, namely, *br*; they all have a meaning connected with bearing or carrying. *Burden* is what is carried; *bier*, what a person is carried on; *barrow*, in wheelbarrow, an implement for carrying things.

No doubt, this is only *prima facie* evidence. We must not forget that we are dealing with a modern language which has passed through many vicissitudes. In order to institute truly scientific comparisons, we should have in each case to trace these words to their Anglo-Saxon, or even to their corresponding Gothic forms.

How great the danger is of trusting to mere similarity of sound in modern languages, you will see at once, if you take the last word *barrow*, which means not only a wheelbarrow, but also a burial-mound. We have only to trace this *barrow* back to its Anglo-Saxon form *beorh*, in order to see that it has nothing to do with bearing or carrying, but that it is connected with the Anglo-Saxon *beorgan*, the German *bergen*, to hide, to protect.

But though it is necessary, before we institute comparisons, always to go back to the oldest forms of words which are within our reach, still for practical purposes it suffices if we know that such words as *bear*, *burden*, *bier*, and *barrow* have all been proved to come from one common source.

And more than this. As *to bear* is used in many languages in the sense of bearing children, we may safely trace to the same source such English words as *birth*, and *bairn*, a child.

Nay, as the same expression is also used of the earth-bearing fruit, we can hardly be wrong in explaining, for instance, *barley*, as what the earth bears or brings forth. In German *Getreide*, M. H. G. *Getregede*, literally, what is born, has become the name of every kind of corn. If we go back to Anglo-Saxon, we find *bær-lic* for barley, in which *lic* is derivative, while *bere* by itself meant barley. In Scotland more particularly *bear* continued to be used for barley, and a coarse kind of barley is still called *bear-barley*. *Barn* also receives its explanation from the same quarter. For *barn* is contracted from *bere-ærn*, which means barley-house, or, as also called, bere-flor.

We have thus collected eight words, which all contain one common element, namely *br*, and which *prima facie* come from the same source. Their various meanings, as we saw, can likewise be traced back to the one fundamental concept of bearing.

From every one of these words ever so many derivatives may be formed, and have been formed.

Think only of the numerous offspring of *to bear*, and the various meanings that can be conveyed by that one word. We have, to bear up, to bear out, to bear oneself, proud bearing, to bear in mind, to bear with, to forbear; then to bear down on a person, in the sense of to press hard on him, to bear away, said of a ship that sails away, to lose one's bearings, bearable, unbearable, a bearer, an office-bearer, bearing in the sense of behavior, child-bearing, and many more.

Now you begin to see how thrifty language can be, and what immense results it can achieve with very small means. It starts with a syllable of two consonants, such as *bar*, and out of it, by means of derivatives, it forms a perfect army of words. If we had a hundred such syllables, and derived only forty words from each, we should possess what, as we found, is wanted for carrying on all social and intellectual intercourse, namely, 4,000 words.

But now we shall be asked, What are those mysterious syllables? What is, for instance, that *bar*, which we discovered as the kernel of ever so many words?

These syllables have been called *roots*. That is, of course, nothing but a metaphorical expression. What is meant is neither more nor less than what you saw just now as the result of our comparison—namely, what remains of a number of words after we separate the purely formative elements. In *bur-den*, *den* is formative: in *birth*, *th* is formative; in *bairn*, *n* is formative. In *barn*, too, *n* is formative, but it is different from the *n* in *bairn*, because it is really a contraction of *ærn*. *Bere-ærn* meant a place for barley, just as *horsern* meant a place for horses, a stable, *slæpern*, a sleeping-place.[1]

There remains therefore *bar* with a variable vowel, and this we call a root, or an ultimate element of speech, because it cannot be analysed any further.

This root *bar*, however, is not an English root. It existed long before English existed, and we find it again in Latin, Greek, Celtic, Slavonic, Zend, and Sanskrit, that is, in all the languages which form what is called the *Aryan family* of speech. As this root *bar* exists in Latin as *fer*, in Greek as *φερ*, in Celtic as *ber*, in Slavonic as *ber*, in Zend as *bar*, and in Sanskrit as bhar, it is clear that it must have existed before these languages separated, and that, as you may imagine, must have been a very, very long time ago.

But you may ask, How did these roots exist? Were they ever independent words, or did they only exist in their derivatives? Of course, it is impossible to answer this question by historical evidence. If anything deserves to be called pre-historic, it is the period of language which precedes the formation of Sanskrit, Greek, and Latin. But if we argue by analogy, we may say that as in Chinese, so in this Proto-Aryan

[1] Morris, *Historical Outlines*, § 322.

language, these roots, without any formative suffixes or prefixes, were probably used by themselves. On the other hand, it is quite true that, as soon as one of these roots was used either as a subject or as a predicate, it had really ceased to be a root in the true sense of that word, and had become a noun, or a verb, or an adjective.

Hitherto, it seems to me, there is nothing difficult, nothing uncertain, nothing mysterious in this process of taking our language to pieces, and separating the radical from the formal elements. It is no more than cracking a nut and separating the kernel from the shell. What the result of this cracking and peeling has been, I shall try to explain to you in my next lecture.

SECOND LECTURE.

THE ANALYSIS OF LANGUAGE.

WE SAW at the end of our last lecture by what process the constituent elements of a language can be discovered. It is a very simple process. You take a word, remove from it all that can be accounted for, that is, all that can be proved to be purely formative and derivative; and what cannot be accounted for, what cannot be further analysed, you accept as an element, as an ultimate fact, or, as scholars are in the habit of calling it, as a root.

Now let me tell you, first of all, that this chemical analysis of words is by no means a new invention. It was performed for the first time more than 2,000 years ago by the grammarians of India. They reduced the whole of their abounding language to about 1,706 roots.[1] Given these roots, they professed to be able to account for every word in Sanskrit, and to a certain extent they achieved it. Considering the time when that experiment was carried out, it strikes us as perfectly marvellous. We, in Europe, were still savages at that time, entirely unacquainted with letters or literature. Still, we have made some advance over

[1] *Science of Language*, Vol. I. p. 306.

Pâṇini, and Mr. Edgren has reduced the number of necessary roots to 816, afterwards to 633, and at last to 587.[1] With these roots he thinks that the great bulk of the Sanskrit vocabulary can be accounted for. And here again we may say that, with certain well-understood exceptions, this promise has been fulfilled. For instance, the root *bar*, or *bhar*, particularly if we include the words derived from Latin *ferre* and adopted in English, such as, for instance, *fertile*, *far* (barley), *farina*, barley-flower, *reference*, *deference*, *conference*, *difference*, *inference*, *preference*, *transference*, and all the rest, would yield more than a hundred English words. We should not want therefore more than a hundred such roots to account for 10,000 words in English. Now, as a matter of fact, the number of Aryan roots which have left offspring in English, is only about 460.[2] When all the offspring of a root dies, of course the root itself comes to an end, and this is what has happened to a number of roots which are required to account for words in Sanskrit, Greek, and Latin, but no longer, for any words existing in English.

It stands to reason that all these statements are broad statements. There is in every language a considerable residue of words which has not yet been traced back to any root. There are likewise many words which are not to be derived from roots at all, but come straight from imitations of sounds, or interjections. To this class belong such words as *cuckoo*, *moo* (cow), *bah* (lamb), *to click*, *to hiss*. The Greeks called the formation of such words *onomatopoeia* or word-manufacturing, by which they meant that they formed a class by themselves, that they were mere

[1] *Science of Thought*, p. 377.

[2] Skeat, *Etymological Dictionary*, pp. 729, seq.

made words, artificial words, not real and natural words, like all the rest.

Besides there are interjections, such as *ah*, *oh*, *fie*, *pooh*, *pah*, and all the rest.

Still, to put the matter broadly—and I cannot here attempt more than to give you the broad outlines of the Science of Language—we have now come to this. Instead of being startled and staggered by 250,000 of words, all crowding in upon us and asking us what they are and whence they came, we are now only confronted by four or five hundred words or roots, and have to render some account of them. If we can do that, the world-old riddle of the origin of language is solved. How from these roots the whole wealth of English was evolved has been shown by Comparative Grammer. Here all formative elements, such as suffixes, prefixes, infixes, all case-terminations, all personal and tense-terminations, have been classified, and traced back, more or less successfully, to so-called demonstrative elements. Here also much remains still to be done, but the broad fact is established once for all, that all we call grammar is the result of synthesis between predicative roots and demonstrative elements, often also between words, ready made.

Thus *birth* was originally *bhar*, to bear, *plus* a demonstrative element *ti*, in English *th*, which localises the act of bearing here and there.

The Sanskrit bi-bhar-mi shows us the same root reduplicated, so as to express continuous action, and followed by mi as a personal demonstrative. *Bearing-I* comes to mean, I bear.

The English *bear-able* is a compound of *bear* with the Roman suffix *able*, the Latin *abilis*, which expresses fitness.

Instances of composition of ready-made words, we have in English in such words as *huzzy*, which stands for *housewife*; or *world*, which stands for *weor* = *man*, and *yld*, age; *god-less*, which means loose or away from God; *god-ly*, which means like God.

We have now to face the final question, What are these roots? If we can answer that, we shall know what language is. We shall not simply stare at it in silent wonderment, nor shall we repeat the old answer that we learnt it from our mother, and our mother from her mother, and thus *ad infinitum*. We shall probably wonder at it all the more, but with an intelligent wonder and pleasure, and not simply with a vacant stare, that so much could have been made out of so little.

All roots which we find in English, in Sanskrit, or rather in that stratum of language which lies even beneath Sanskrit, are perfectly definite in sound. Their consonants are guttural, dental, or labial, surd, sonant, or aspirated. These consonants can be modified according to certain rules, but they are not vague and indefinite, as is often the case with the vowels and consonants of less developed languages.

Secondly, they nearly all express acts, such as bearing, striking, pushing, cutting, tearing. And you will find, if you trace even the most abstract and elevated notions back to their original source, they are borrowed from such material concepts as tearing, pushing, and all the rest. *Abstract*, for instance, is what is torn away, *elevated* what is pushed aloft.

Thirdly, they are all conceptual, that is to say they do not express a single percept, as, for instance, the sound of *cuckoo*, or *moo*, or *bah*, but they signify acts, or qualities, conceived as the result of acts. *Percept*, as you know, is the technical name given to our cognisance of a single object actually perceived by the senses; while concept is the technical term for our cognisance of something common to several objects, which can never by itself be conceived by the senses. Thus *snow* is called a percept, the *white* of snow a concept.

When logicians ask, how we came to form concepts, they seem to see no difficulty whatever in this process. There was *white* in snow, they say, in chalk, and in milk; and the sign for this common quality was the sound *white*. So, no doubt, it is with us; but in the evolution of the human mind, the forming of concepts represents quite a new epoch, and like everything else in that evolution, we must try to discover some natural necessity for it. Now the first natural necessity for our taking cognisance of two or more percepts as one, lies in our own acts. Most of our acts are repeated acts. We do not strike, or push, or rub once only, but repeatedly. This consciousness, therefore, of our own repeated acts as one action, grew by necessity into our first conceptual knowledge, and that primitive conceptual knowledge is embodied in those very roots which, as we saw, were the feeders of all human speech. When this conceptual tendency was once started, it would go on growing stronger with every new generation, till at last our whole intellectual life became, as it now is, conceptual. It is the beginning of this peculiar mental operation that has to be explained, and it should be explained, if possible, as brought about by the same natural necessity which forces us to see and to hear. I do not say that the consciousness of our own repeated acts is the only possible way in which the beginning of concepts can be explained. All I say is that it is the most natural explanation, and that it is confirmed in the most unexpected way by the facts of language.

One more question now remains. Why should the consciousness of our acts be accompanied by certain definite sounds, such as *bhar*, to bear, *mar*, to rub, *stâ*, to stop, *tan*, to stretch? Here again our answer can only be hypothetical. Often though we cannot drive our shaft into a deep geological stratum, we can guess by analogy what its constituent elements must have been. It is the same in the geology of language.

With regard to the sounds accompanying our notions, we know from physiology that under any strong muscular effort it is a relief to the system to let our breath come out strongly and repeatedly, and by that process to let the vocal cords vibrate in different ways. That is the case with savages, and it is the case even with us. These natural sounds accompanying our acts are called *clamor concomitans*. Navvies when they have to lift a heavy weight together, shout *Yo heo*. Sailors, when they pull together, have their own monotonous song. Even children, when they march or dance, break out naturally in some kind of rhythmic singsong. Here we have at all events a hint,—for I will say no more,—how this natural music which accompanied the acts of early people, this *clamor concomitans*, could have supplied the outward signs of the inward concepts of these acts. What we want are natural signs of concepts, not of percepts. If our thoughts and our language consisted of percepts only, the sound of *cuckoo* for the cuckoo, of *moo* for cow, and *bah* for lamb would have been amply sufficient. But we must take language as it is. Language as it is, is derived from sounds which express the consciousness of our acts, and which are *ipso facto* conceptual. Such sounds can be supplied, as it seems to me, through one channel only, namely, from the sounds which accompany our acts, and particularly such acts as are performed in common with our fellow-men. From the fact that these primitive acts were performed in common, another advantage arises, namely, that the sounds which accompany them, and which afterwards are to remind us of them, are naturally understood by others as well as by ourselves, in every part of the world where a beginning of social life is made.

Let us see now what are the results at which we have arrived, not by *a priori* theories about language and thought, but by a mere analysis of facts, of the facts of language, as garnered in our dictionaries and grammars.

We found that a small number of insignificant little syllables, such as *bhar*, or *dhar*, or *mar*, or *pat*, or *man* formed the elements with which the whole English language had been put together. We found that a somewhat larger number sufficed to account for the whole verbal harvest of all the Aryan languages, such as Sanskrit, Persian, Greek, Latin, Russian, German, and Welsh. I may add that a similar analysis of the Semitic languages, such as Hebrew, Syriac, and Arabic has led to exactly the same result, and that in other families of languages also, outside the pale of Aryan and Semitic, something corresponding to our roots has been discovered as the residue of a careful etymological analysis.

We may now with perfect safety make another step in advance.

These so-called roots, these insignificant little syllables, which form the foundation of all that we call language, form at the same time the impassable barrier between man and beast. Whatever animals may be able to do—and no one who has watched intelligent animals without preconceived opinions, can doubt that they can do almost everything that we do, only in their own way—but whatever the cleverest animals are able to do, they cannot form these little syllables as signs of concepts. And as what we mean by a concept cannot come into existence except by a sign, we may argue, with a certain amount of plausibility, that animals have not what we call concepts, and that this is the true reason why they have not what we mean by language. It may seem a very small matter, this being able to use a number of syllables as signs of concepts; but it forms nevertheless the *sine quâ non* of language, and no one will venture to say that language is a small matter, even though it consists at first of 300 words only. The first rays of language, like the first rays of the dawn, change the world from night to day, from darkness to light, from a strange phantom into our own home. However humble we may try to be, no one who really knows what language means, and what it has done for us, will be able to persuade himself that, after all, there is not a radical difference between him and the parrot, the elephant, or the ape.

Here then, is one of the lessons which the Science of Language teaches us. It opens our eyes at first to the marvellousness of language, and makes us see that the language which we speak, and which seems to us so very simple, so very natural, so very familiar, is really something so magnificent, so wonderful, so different from everything else we have or do or know, that some of the wisest of mankind could not help themselves, but had to ascribe it to a divine source.

It shows us secondly, that, like all the most marvellous things, language also, if carefully studied, discloses a simplicity more wonderful even than its supposed complexity. As chemistry has shown us that the whole universe, the sea and the mountains, the earth and the sun, the trees and the animals, the simplest protoplasm and the most highly organised brain, are all put together with about sixty simple substances, Comparative Philology has taught us that with about 400 simple radical substances, and a few demonstrative elements, the names and the knowledge of the whole universe have been elaborated. Only by being named does this universe become our universe, and all our knowledge, the accumulation of the labor of countless generations, is possible only because it could be handed down to us in the sacred shrine of language. Let us be humble, as much as you like; but on the other hand, let us not depreciate our inheritance. We have not made our language ourselves, we have received it. We are what we are by what those who came before us have done for us. Like the coral islands which have been built up by the silent and self-sacrificing industry of millions of millions of living beings, our languages have been elaborated by the incessant labors of millions of millions of those who came before us. Whether those ancestors of ours were hairy, whether they had tails, whether they walked on all fours, or whether they climbed trees—what does that matter to us? Our body is a mere conglomerate of cells. It comes and goes, it is born and dies. It is not ours, it is not our own self. But whatever these prehistoric ancestors of ours may have been, they were able to bring to maturity and to compound in ever-varying forms those intellectual cells which, for want of a better name, we call roots, and which constitute a barrier between ourselves and all other living beings—a barrier which fortunately does not vanish by being ignored. The Science of Language, better than any other science, teaches us our true position in the world. Our bodily frame is like the bodily frame of the animals; it is even less perfect than that of many animals. We are beasts, we are wild beasts, and those who have fought with wild beasts, not only at Ephesus, but within the arena of their own hearts, are least likely to forget that lesson. But there is a light within us, which not only lights up our own true self, but throws its rays upon the whole world that surrounds and holds us. That light is language. Take away that language, and man is lower than the dumb animals of the field and of the forest. Give us that language, and we are not only higher than all animals, but lifted up into a new world, thinking thoughts and speaking words which the animal may obey, may even imitate, but which no animal can ever create, or even impart to its own offspring.

THE LESSON TAUGHT BY THE SCIENCE OF LANGUAGE.

I have tried hitherto to show how the Science of Language teaches us our true position with regard to animals. Let me now try to explain to you how the same science has taught us likewise our true position with regard to our fellow-men.

I mentioned before that English belongs to what I call the Aryan family of speech. That means that in the same manner as Italian, French, and Spanish are derived from Latin, English and the other Aryan languages are derived from a more ancient language, which is lost, but which must once have had a very real historical existence. This lost language we call *Aryan*, or *Proto-Aryan.* The descendants of the Proto-Aryan language are known to us in seven great branches, called the *Teutonic*, the *Celtic*, the *Italic*, the *Greek*, the *Slavonic*, the *Iranic*, and the *Indic.* The first five constitute the *North-Western* or *European*, the other two the *South-Eastern* or *Asiatic division.*

Now let us consider for a moment what all this means. English belongs to the Teutonic branch of the Aryan family; that means that English, and German, and Dutch, and Danish, and Swedish, and even Icelandic, are all varieties of one type of Aryan speech, and that all the people who speak these languages are held together by the closest ties of a linguistic relationship.

It is said that blood is thicker than water, but it may be said with even greater truth that language is thicker than blood. If, in the interior of Africa, surrounded by black men, whose utterances are utterly unintelligible, we suddenly met with a man who could speak English, we should care very little whether he was English, or Irish, or American. We should understand him, and be able to exchange our thoughts with him. That brings us together far more closely than if we met a Welshman speaking nothing but Welsh, or a Scotchman speaking nothing but Gaelic; or, for all that, an Englishman who, having been brought up in China, could speak nothing but Chinese. A common language is a common bond of intellectual brotherhood, far stronger than any supposed or real community of blood. Common blood without a common language leaves us as perfect strangers. A common language, even without common blood, makes the whole world feel akin.

It is quite true that the different Teutonic dialects have changed so much, that at present an Englishman can hardly understand a Dutchman, a Dutchman can hardly understand a German, while to a German, Danish and Swedish and Icelandic sound as strange as French and Italian. Nevertheless, in spite of dynastic and national feuds, English, Dutch, Germans, Danes, and Swedes, feel themselves as one, when brought face to face with Slavonic or Romanic nations. They know that by their language, if not by their blood, they represent a unity in the history of the world. The same feeling is shared most strongly by all Slavonic people. However much they may be separated from each other by government, religion, and general civilisation, against Teutonic nations the Slaves are one. There can be no doubt, however, that during the middle ages, and also in modern times, the mixture of blood between Slaves and Germans has been enormous. The Slavonic names of places and families in Germany, and the German names of places and families in Bohemia, Poland, and Russia tell their own tale. Nevertheless, a man who speaks Bohemian, Polish, or Russian, feels himself a Slave; a man who speaks German feels himself a German, and he can hardly understand what is meant when he is told that the blood of his great-grandfather was either Slavonic or Teutonic. Nor do I think that any biologist has as yet given us a scientific definition of what is meant by Slavonic or Teutonic blood, by Slavonic or Teutonic hair, or skulls, or skin; and until that is done, such undefined words should simply be boycotted in all scientific discussions.

The Science of Language, however, professes to teach us something else. Whatever the so-called national antipathy between people speaking Slavonic and Teutonic and Romanic languages may be, they have now to learn a new lesson—a lesson that may bear good fruit in the future, namely, that these very Slavonic, Teutonic, and Romanic languages, which at present divide the people who speak them, belong to one and the same family, and were once spoken by the common ancestors of these divided and sometimes hostile nations.

At present such lessons may seem to possess a scientific interest only, in so far as they have made scholars take a completely new view of the ancient history of mankind. The old idea that our languages were all derived from Hebrew, has been surrendered long ago; but it was not surrendered without an effort, an effort almost as great as that which made the world surrender its faith in the central position of the earth.

After that came a new surrender, of which I still remember the beginning and the end. I myself was brought up in the most straitest school of classical scholarship. I was led to believe that there were only two so-called classical languages in the world—Greek and Latin—and that all the other nations of Europe were more or less of barbarians till they were debarbarised by contact with Greek and Roman civilisation. That the language of the ancient Germans or Celts could have been anything but an uncouth jargon, as compared with the language of Homer and Virgil; that the grammar of the Goths could have been as perfect as that of the Hellenes; that the natives of Gaul and Germany could have possessed a religion, a mythology, and an epic poetry that could be compared to the religion, the mythology, and the epic poetry of Greeks and Romans—these are ideas which would have been scouted by all scholars, in fact by all educated people, at the beginning of our century. But facts will have their way, however much they may be scouted at first. That the Gothic language was as finely organised as Latin, admitted of no contradiction. That the religion and the mythology of the Teutonic nations flowed from the same source as the religion and mythology of the Greeks and Romans, had to be granted even by the best Greek and Latin scholars of the day, such as Gottfried Hermann, Otfried Müller, and Welcker. And that the epic poetry of Iceland, and of Germany, the Edda and the Nibelunge, contained fragments of as peculiar beauty as the Homeric poems, was freely acknowledged by the foremost poets and critics in Germany, such as Herder and Goethe.

Though no one would have denied the superiority of the Greek genius, and though the glory of having raised the world from darkness to light will forever remain with the Greeks, yet the Greeks, and their pupils, the Romans, could no longer command a position apart from all the rest. They had made a better use of the talent committed to them; it may be they had received from the beginning a richer endowment. But those whom in their pride they had called barbarians, had now to be recognised as of the same kith and kin from the beginning, nay, destined hereafter to outstrip even their masters in the historic race after the true, the noble, and the good. Classical scholars who can remember the events of the last fifty years know best how radical a change every branch of classical learning has undergone, when it became possessed by this new comparative spirit.

Like many movements, true in themselves, this movement also has sometimes been carried too far. No one, it was boldly asserted, could know Greek who did not know Sanskrit or Gothic. No one could understand Roman mythology who had not studied modern folk-lore. All this is true in a certain sense, but it has been much exaggerated. Still, our historical horizon has been permanently enlarged. Greeks and Romans have been placed in a new historical environment, and so far from losing in their prestige, they only stand forth in bolder relief by the historical background with which the Science of Language has supplied them.

But if this feeling of fraternity between the principal languages of Europe can only claim a scientific and literary interest, it has produced very practical results in other quarters. The feeling between the white and the black man is deeply engrained in human nature, and in spite of all the arguments in support of our common humanity, it was not to be wondered at that the dark people of India should look upon their white conquerors as strangers, and that the white rulers of India should treat their dark subjects almost as people of another kind. That feeling seemed wellnigh unconquerable, till the discovery of Sanskrit proved beyond all manner of doubt that the languages spoken by the inhabitants of India must have sprung from the same source as Greek, Latin, and English. The name *Indo-European* marked not only a new epoch in the study of language; it ushered in a new period in the history of the world. Language, as I said before, is thicker than blood, and while a so-called community of blood conveys really no definite meaning at all, a community of language that extended even to consonants, vowels, and accents, proved an intellectual fraternity far stronger than any merely genealogical relationship.

When the Hindus learnt for the first time that their ancient language, the Sanskrit, was closely connected with Greek and Latin, and with that uncouth jargon spoken by their rulers, they began to feel a pride in their language and their descent, and they ceased to look upon the pale-skinned strangers from the North as strange creatures from another, whether a better or a worse, world. They felt what we feel when later in life we meet with a man whom we had quite forgotten. But as soon as he tells us that he was at the same school with ourselves, as soon as he can remind us of our common masters, or repeat some of the slang terms of our common childhood and youth, he becomes a schoolfellow, a fellow, a man whom we seem to know, though we do not even recollect his name. Neither the English nor the Hindus recollected their having been at the same school together thousands of years ago, but the mere fact of their using the same slang words, such as mâtar and *mother*, such as bhrâtar and *brother*, such as staras and *stars*, was sufficient to convince them that most likely they had been in the same scrapes and had been flogged by the same masters. It was not so much that either the one or the other party felt very much raised in their own eyes by this discovery, as that a feeling sprang up between them that, after all, they might be chips of the same block. I could give you ever so many proofs in support of this assertion, at all events on the part of the Hindus, and likewise from the speeches of some of the most enlightened rulers of India. But as I might seem to be a not altogether unprejudiced witness in such a matter, I prefer to quote the words of an eminent American scholar, Mr. Horatio Hale. "When the people of Hindostan in the last century," he writes, "came under the British power, they were regarded as a debased and alien race. Their complexion reminded their conquerors of Africa. Their divinities were hideous monsters. Their social system was anti-human and detestable. Suttee, Thuggee, Juggernaut, all sorts of cruel and shocking abominations seemed to characterise and degrade them. The proudest Indian prince was, in the sight and ordinary speech of the rawest white subaltern, only a 'nigger.' This universal contempt was retorted with a hatred as universal, and threatening in the future most disastrous consequences to the British rule. Then came an unexpected and wonderful discovery. European philologists, studying the language of the conquered race, discovered that the classic mother-tongue of Northern Hindostan was the elder sister of the Greek, the Latin, the German, and the Celtic languages. At the same time a splendid literature was unearthed, which filled the scholars of Europe with astonishment and delight. The despised Asiatics became not only the blood-relations, but the teachers and exemplars, of their conquerors. The revulsion of feeling on both sides was immense. Mutual esteem and confidence, to a large extent, took the place of repulsion and distrust. Even in the mutiny which occurred while the change was yet in progress, a very large proportion of the native princes and people refused to take part in the outbreak. Since that time, good-will has steadily grown with the fellowship of common studies and aims. It may freely be affirmed, at this day, that *the discovery of the Sanskrit language and literature has been of more value to England in the retention and increase of her Indian Empire, than an army of a hundred thousand men.*"

This is but one out of many lessons which the Science of Language has taught us. We have become familiarised with many of these lessons, and are apt to forget that not more than fifty years ago they were scouted as absurd by the majority of classical scholars, while they have proved to be the discovery of a new world, or, if you like, the recovery of an old world.

But there are many more lessons which that science has still in store for us. There is still much gold and silver to be raised by patient labor from the mines that have been opened. What is wanted are patient and honest laborers, and it is in the hope of gaining fresh recruits that I have ventured to invite you to listen to my pleading.

THIRD LECTURE.

THOUGHT THICKER THAN BLOOD.

I HAVE been asked the question, a very natural question, and one that has often been discussed since the discovery of Sanskrit and since the establishment of a close relationship between Sanskrit, Persian, Greek, Latin, Russian, German, English, and Welsh—Does the close relationship of these languages prove a real relationship between the people who speak these languages?

At first sight, the answer seems very easy. As a negro may learn English and become, as has been the case, an English bishop, it would seem as if language by itself could hardly be said to prove relationship. That being so, I have always, beginning with my very first contribution to the Science of Language—my letter to Bunsen "On the Turanian Languages," published in 1854—I have always, I say, warned against mixing up these two relationships,—the relationship of language and the relationship of blood. As these warnings, however, have been of very little avail, I venture to repeat them once more, and in the very words which I used in the year 1854:—

"Much of the confusion of terms and indistinctness of principles, both in ethnology and philology, is due to the combined study of these heterogeneous sciences. Ethnological race and linguistic race are not commensurate, except in ante-historical times, or perhaps at the very dawn of history. With the migrations of tribes, their wars, their colonies, their conquests and alliances, which, if we may judge from their effects, must have been much more violent in the ethnic than ever in the political periods of history, it is impossible to imagine that ethnological race and linguistic race should continue to run parallel. The physiologist should therefore pursue his own science, unconcerned about language. Let him see how far the skulls, or the hair, or the color, or the skin of different tribes admit of classification; but to the sound of their words his ear should be as deaf as that of the ornithologist must be to the notes of caged birds. If his Caucasian race includes nations or individuals speaking Aryan (Greek), Turanian (Turkish), and Semitic (Hebrew) languages, it is not his fault. His system must not be altered in order to suit another system. There is a better solution both for his difficulties and for those of the philologist than mutual compromise. The philologist should collect his evidence, arrange his classes, divide and combine, as if no Blumenbach had ever looked at skulls, as if no Camper had ever measured facial angles, as if no Owen had examined the basis of a cranium. His evidence is the evidence of language, and nothing else; this he must follow, even though it were in the teeth of history, physical or political. Would he scruple to call the language of England Teutonic, and class it with the Low-German dialects, because the physiologist could tell him that the skull, the bodily habitat of such language, is of a Celtic type, or because the genealogist can prove that the arms of the family conversing in this idiom are of Norman origin? With the philologist English is Teutonic, and nothing but Teutonic. Ethnological suggestions as to an early substratum of Celtic inhabitants in Britain, or historical information as to a Norman conquest, will always be thankfully received by the philologist; but if every record were burnt, and every skull pulverised, the spoken language of the present day alone would enable the philologist to say that English, as well as Dutch and Frisian, belongs to the Low-German branch—that this branch, together with the High-German and Scandinavian, belongs to the Teutonic stock, and that this stock, together with the Celtic, Slavonic, Hellenic, Italic, Iranic, and Indic, belongs to the Aryan family. . . .

"There ought to be no compromise of any sort between ethnological and philological science. It is only by stating the glaring contradictions between the two sciences that truth can be elicited. . . . Ever since Blumenbach tried to establish his five races of men (Caucasian, Mongolian, American, Ethiopian, and Malay), which Cuvier reduced to three (Caucasian, Ethiopian, and Mongolian), while Prichard raised them to seven (Iranian, Turanian, American, Hottentots, Negroes, Papuas, and Alfourous), it was felt that these physiological classifications could not be brought to harmonise with the evidence of language. . . . This point was never urged with sufficient strength till at last Humboldt, in his *Kosmos* (I., 353), stated it as a plain fact, that, even from a physiological point of view, it is impossible to recognise in the groups of Blumenbach any true typical distinction, any general and consistent natural principle. From a physiological point of view, we may speak of varieties of man,—no longer of races, if that term is to mean more than variety. Physiologically the unity of the human species is a fact established as firmly as the unity of any other animal species. So much then, but no more, the philologist should learn from the physiologist. He should know that in the present state of physiological science it is impossible to admit more than one beginning of the human race. He should bear in mind that Man is a species, created once, and divided in none of its varieties by specific distinctions; in fact, that the common origin of the Negro and the Greek admits of as little doubt as that of the poodle and the greyhound. . . ."

I have made this long extract from a book written by me in 1854, because it will show how strongly I have always deprecated the mixing up of Ethnology and Philology, and likewise that I was a Darwinian long before Darwin. At that time, however, I still entertained a hope that the physiologist might succeed in framing a real classification of races, on the evidence of skulls, or the skin, or the hair, as the philologist has succeeded in framing a real classification of languages, on the evidence of grammar. But in this hope we have been disappointed. Mankind has proved obstreperous; it has not allowed itself to be classified. According to Darwin, all men form but one species, and to his mind that species overlaps even the limits usually assigned to mankind. So far there seems to be at present a general agreement among physiologists. But all further attempts at classifying the human species have signally failed. Some biologists (Virey) have proposed two classes; Cuvier proposed three, Linnaeus four, Blumenbach five, Buffon six, Prichard and Peschel seven, Agassiz eight, Pickering eleven, Friedrich Müller twelve, Bory de St. Vincent fifteen, Morton twenty-two, Crawford sixty, and Burke sixty-three.[1] This does not prove that all these classifications are wrong. One of them may possibly hereafter be proved to be right. But at present not only is there the most decided disagreement among the most eminent biologists, but some of them, and these men of high authority in biological science, have themselves given up the whole problem of classifying mankind on physiological grounds as utterly hopeless. Oscar Peschel, in his classical work, *The Races of Man and Their Geographical Distribution*, sums up his conclusions in the following words: "We must needs confess that neither the shape of the skull nor any other portion of the skeleton has afforded distinguishing marks of the human races; that the color of the skin likewise displays only various gradations of darkness; and that the hair alone comes to the aid of our systematic attempts, and even this not always, and never with sufficient decisiveness. . . . Who then can presume to talk of the immutability of racial types? To base a classification of the human race on the character of the hair only, as Haeckel has done, was a hazardous venture, and could but end as all other artificial systems have ended."

[1] Horatio Hale, *Race and Language*, p. 340.

Nor does Peschel stand alone in this honest confession that all classification of the human race based on the color of the skin, the texture of the hair, the shape of the skull, has completely failed. No one has of late done more excellent work in ethnology than the indefatigable Director of the American Bureau of Ethnology, Major Powell. Yet this is what he says[1]: "There is a science of anthropology, composed of subsidiary sciences. There is a science of sociology, which includes all the institutions of mankind. There is a science of philology, which includes the languages of mankind. And there is a science of philosophy, which includes the opinions of mankind. But there is no science of ethnology, for the attempt to classify mankind in groups has failed on every hand."

The very Nestor among ethnologists, Horatio Hale, from whose essay on "Race and Language"[2] I have largely quoted, has, after a long life devoted to ethnological and linguistic studies, arrived at exactly the same conclusion, and expressed it with the same openness, that the classification of mankind cannot be founded on color, hair, or skull, but must be founded on language.

This is, no doubt, a great collapse. We had all been brought up with a belief in a white, a yellow, a brown, a red, and a black race; or, if we entered more deeply into the subject, we seemed perfectly certain of a Caucasian, Mongolian, American, Ethiopian, and Malay race. More recently, the division of the human race according to the texture of their hair, as proposed by Haeckel and adopted by Friedrich

1 *Science*, June 24, 1887.
2 *Popular Science Review*, January, 1888.

Müller in his learned work on Ethnology, was accepted by the new school of ethnologists as meeting all objections that had been made to former classifications. Still, it is far better to confess that no satisfactory classification has as yet been discovered, than to maintain that hair, color, and shape of skulls have proved real criteria of racial distinction. It does not follow by any means that further research may not bring to light a real divisor of the human race. At present, however, color of skin is in conflict with shape of skull, and shape of skull is in conflict with texture of hair. What we want is a principle of division that shall do justice to most, if not to all, the essential qualities of the varieties of man, provided always that such essential qualities can be discovered.

Till this is done, I agree with Mr. Horatio Hale that the most satisfactory, nay the only possible division of the human race, is that which is based on language. No one doubts that languages can be classified, and that the true principle of classification is their grammar. If some languages stand as yet apart, which hereafter may be proved to be related, or if other languages have not as yet been analysed at all, that does not interfere with the enormous area of human speech which has been carefully surveyed. It is, of course, of that area alone that we can make any assertion, and our assertion is that the people who speak the same or cognate languages may, nay must, be treated as closely related. In modern times the frequent intercourse between all the people of the world, and the facility with which foreign languages may be acquired, are apt to make us look upon language as something, not essential, but purely accidental. But that was not the case in ancient times; and though the acquisition of a foreign language may be accidental, language as such is not. It is language that makes man. Language is surely more of the essence of man than his skin, or his color, or his skull, or his hair. Blood, flesh, and bone are not of our true essence. They are in a constant flux, and change with every year, till at last they return to the dust. Our body is our uniform, very tight sometimes, very painful to don, very painful to doff, but still our uniform only. It matters very little whether it is black or white. Language, on the contrary, is the very embodiment of our true self. Take away language, and we shall indeed be mere animals, and no more. And, besides that, it is language that binds individuals together into families, clans, and nations, and survives them all in its constant growth, thus enabling us to base our classification on general and permanent characteristics, and not on peculiarities which, for all we know, may be the result of climate, diet, and heredity.

There can be no doubt that in the beginning at all events, the members of one family spoke one and the same language. When families grew into clans and nations, they would continue to speak the same language, and if colonies started from their original home, they could not but carry the same language with them.

But it is objected, that in the spreading of nations a mixture would necessarily occur between, say, white and black tribes.

No doubt it would, and it is for this very reason that physiological classification breaks down, while linguistic classification, though it becomes more difficult, does not become impossible. After blood has once become mixed, no scientific test has yet been discovered for distinguishing its ingredients. No one can tell, for instance, whether the offspring of a white man and a black woman should be classed as Caucasian or as Negro. The color may be quite white or quite black, or something between the two. The nose and mouth may be Negro-like, and yet the color may be fair, and the shape of the skull and the texture of the hair may be Caucasian. After one or two generations certain varieties may either become permanent, or they may, by the force of atavism, return to their original type. New mixtures of mixed or mongrel offspring with other mongrel or with pure breeds will make confusion even worse confounded, and after hundreds and thousands of years, the very possibility of pure breeds may very justly be doubted. How then should we dare in our days to classify mankind according to such variable peculiarities as color, skull, or hair?

The case is very different with regard to languages. No doubt, while this social intercourse between black and white people takes place, the white might adopt some words from the black, and the black from the white people. But these words could nearly always be distinguished, as we are able to distinguish French, Latin, and Greek words imbedded in English. And there would always remain the criterion of grammar, which enables us to say that English is and remains a Teutonic language, even though every word in an English sentence should be, as it often is, of Latin origin.

Lastly, it should never be forgotten, that if we speak of Âryas, we mean no more than the speakers of Aryan languages. As to their color, skull, or hair, we neither assert nor imply anything, unless we happen to know it from other sources. We may thus use "languages" as a synonym of "people," just as Nebuchadnezzar addressed his subjects, "O people, nations, and languages." It is quite possible—in fact, it is almost inevitable in the constant turmoil of history—that the same language may come to be spoken by the white and the black, or any other variety of man. We take that for granted, and we should always have to make allowance for it, whenever we have to make any assertions as to the physical appearance of the Aryan or Semitic or Turanian speakers. But even then there remains the fact that, whenever there is a mixture of language, there is at the same time a much greater mixture of blood; and while it is possible to analyse mixed language by scientific tests, no tests whatever have as yet been discovered for analysing mixed blood. It would be very hazardous to say that hereafter such tests may not be discovered, and that a classification of the human race according to physiological peculiarities is altogether impossible. What I maintain is that all attempts *hitherto made* have failed, and that if we want to classify the species to which we belong, we can only do it on linguistic grounds.

Much fault has been found with a remark which I made many years ago, that the same blood runs in the veins of the Sepoy and of the English soldier, that they are brothers in blood as well as brothers-in-arms. And yet, though it is difficult to prove it in every single case, all speaks in favor of supposing that the soldier who speaks English and the soldier who speaks Bengâlî, must be descended from ancestors who in far distant times spoke the same language and shared the same blood. There may be Sepoys of Mongolian origin; but though of course I did not mean them, yet the probability is that even they, if they have learned to speak an Indian vernacular, are descended from ancestors who intermarried with women of Aryan origin. As a rule, no tribe, whether conquered or conquering, adopts the language of the conquerors or the conquered, and abstains at the same time from intermarriage. And what one single marriage may produce can easily be shown. Let there be one couple of a black man and a white woman, and suppose they have four children, two boys and two girls. Let those boys and girls marry outsiders, whatever their color may be. Then, if each of these four couples has again four children, there would be sixteen mongrels. In another twenty years these sixteen might produce thirty-two, and in another twenty years these thirty-two might have produced a total of sixty-four mongrels. If this process is carried on at the same not very extravagant ratio of four children to every couple, about six hundred years would suffice to produce a population of 2,147,483,648 human beings, all mongrels. This, I believe, is a great deal more than the population of the whole earth, which is said to amount to no more than 1,400,000,000. If we ask what the language of all these people would be, the answer is easy. It would be the language of one of their two ancestors, and it need not differ from that language more than the English of to-day differs from that of Robert of Gloucester. But however much it differed, we could always discover whether the grammar, the lifeblood of their language, was like that of the Negroes or like that of the Greeks. With regard to color, skull, and hair, however, it would be impossible to hazard any conjecture. If the original white man and black woman were only varieties of a common type, and their color was due to climatic influences, their offspring might be neither black nor white, but any color—grey, brown, or red. The noses of their descendants might be Greek or Negro-like, their skulls dolichocephalic or brachycephalic, their hair straight, or curled, or tufty.

It was necessary to enter into this subject more fully, because, whether from a dislike of the idea that the same blood might run in the veins of the Sepoy and of the English soldier, or from some other cause, the idea of an Indo-European humanity has often been scouted, and our ancestors have been sought for in every part of the world rather than somewhere in Asia. You will now understand in what sense Indo-European speech is equivalent with Indo-European race, and how far we are justified with Nebuchadnezzar to use languages as synonymous with nations.

It may be that the practical usefulness of the lesson taught us by the Science of Lauguage, that all Âryas do not only speak the same tongue, but are children of the same parents, is at present confined to the dark inhabitants of India and their fair rulers who came from the extreme West of Europe. But in time to come the same lesson may revive older and deeper sympathies between all Indo-European nations, even between those who imagine that they are divided, if not by language, at all events by blood.

The Celts of Ireland are Âryas, and speak to them only the language of the Aryan brotherhood, and the wild fancies of a separate Fenian blood will soon vanish.

The French are Âryas, and more than that, they are, to a very considerable extent, Franks, and their veins are as full of the best Teutonic blood as their language is of the best Teutonic speech. Why should the French and the Germans not learn again those neighborly sentiments which have made the westward march of the Aryan brotherhood the triumphal progress of true civilisation?

The Slaves are Âryas, and so far as they are Âryas, tillers of the soil, (for that is the original meaning of the word,) they have preserved some of the noblest features of the Aryan race. Why should they be taught to look upon their German neighbors as aliens and enemies, when they have so many interests and so many duties in common? Why should there be strife between their herdmen, when they know that they are brethren, and there is land enough for all of them, on the right and on the left?

These may seem but idle dreams, of little interest to the practical politician. All I can say is, I wish it were so. But my memory reaches back far enough to make me see the real and lasting mischief for which, I fear, the Science of Language has been responsible for the last fifty years. The ideas of race and nationality, founded on language, have taken such complete possession of the fancy both of the young and the old, that all other arguments seem of no avail?

Why was Italy united? Because the Italian language embodied Italian nationality. Why was Germany united? Because of Arndt's song, What is the German's Fatherland? and the answer given, As far as sounds the German tongue. Why is Russia so powerful a centre of attraction for the Slavonic inhabitants of Turkey and Germany? Because the Russian language, even though it is hardly understood by Servians, Croatians, and Bulgarians, is known to be most closely allied. Even from the mere cinders of ancient dialects, such as Welsh, Gaelic, and Erse, eloquent agitators know how to fan a new, sometimes a dangerous, fire.

But if the Science of Language has encouraged these various national aspirations in places even where separation and national independence would mean political annihilation; if it has called forth a spirit of separatism, it has also another lesson to teach, that of an older, a higher, a truer brotherhood—a lesson too often forgotten, when the opposite lesson seems better to answer political ends. As dialects may well exist by the side of a national speech, nay, as they form a constant supply of life, and vigor, and homely grace to the classical language, so imperial rule does not exclude provincial independence, but may derive from the various members of a great empire, if only held under proper control, its best strength, its permanent health, and that delightful harmony which is the reward of all true and unselfish statesmanship.

THE CRADLE OF THE ÂRYAS.

And now let us return once more from the present and the future to the most distant past. If we are all members of the great Aryan brotherhood, the question whence the Âryas came, and what was the original Aryan home, was a natural and legitimate subject of a scholar's curiosity. The question was asked and answered without much hesitation, though, of course, with a clear knowledge that the answer could be speculative only. Traditions among the South-Eastern Âryas, the Indians and Persians, might point to the North, the legends of North-Western Âryas, the Greeks and Germans, might point to the North or the East, as their earthly paradise; but such dreams would be of little help in settling events supposed to have taken place two, three, it may be four or five thousand years before the beginning of our era. The only arguments, if arguments they can be called, or, we should rather say, the only impressions by which scholars were guided in giving a guess at the whereabouts of the cradle of the Aryan race, were first of all *geological*, and afterwards *semi-historical*. Geology tells us that the first regions inhabitable by human beings were the high plateau of Pamir in the Belurtagh, and the chain of the Caucasus between the Caspian, the Black Sea, and the Mediterranean. No geologist would ever think of any part of Europe as inhabited, or inhabitable, at the same period of time as these two highest points in Asia. From the same high plateau spring the rivers Oxus and Yaxartes, which would have served as guides to the West and the North-West, and the Indus, which would have served as a guide to the South-East; the former leading the Indo-European race to Europe, the latter to India.

And when we leave these distant geological periods, we find again all the beginnings of what we may call civilised life in Asia. I say nothing of China, or Babylon and Assyria, of Egypt, Phenicia, and Palestine. All these countries were teeming with civilised life when, so far as history tells us anything, Europe may still have been a sheet of ice, a swamp, or a howling wilderness. But if we confine our attention to the Âryas, we find them entering the land of the

Seven Rivers, as they called the country of the Panjâb, at a time when Europe had hardly risen above the horizon of legend, much less of history. If we claimed no more than 1000 B. C. as the date of that Aryan immigration into India, the language which they brought with them presupposes untold centuries for its growth. When we proceed to Media and Persia, we find there, too, traces of an ancient language and literature, closely allied with that of India; and we can watch how in historical times these Medes and Persians are brought in contact with an even more ancient civilisation in Babylon, in Egypt, and in Phenicia. When that Median and Persian wave rolls on to Asia Minor, and after the conquest of the Ionian settlements there, threatens to overwhelm Europe, it is repelled by the Greeks, whose civilisation was then of a comparatively recent date. And when, after the Persian wars, the stream of Greek civilisation flows westward to Italy, and from Italy overflows into Gaul and Germany, sweeping everything before it, it meets there with hardly any monuments of ancient growth, and with no evidence of a language more primitive than Sanskrit, or of a literature and religion to be compared for freshness and simplicity with the religious literature of the Vedic age.

It might have been intelligible if, under these circumstances, the cradle of the Aryan race had been sought for in India or Persia, possibly even in Asia Minor, in Greece, or in Italy. But to place that cradle in the untrodden forests of Germany, or even on the shores of the bleak Scandinavian peninsula, would seem to have required a courage beyond the reach of ordinary mortals.

Yet, this feat has been accomplished by some German ethnologists, and the south coast of Sweden has actually been singled out as the hive from which the Âryas swarmed, not only into Germany, Italy, Greece, and Armenia, but into Persia and India likewise. Scholars shook their heads and rubbed their eyes, but they were told that this counted for nothing, and that the least they could do was to prove that Sweden had *not* been the original home of the Âryas. Now, you know how difficult it is under all circumstances to prove a negative; but in this case it became doubly difficult, because there was hardly anything adduced that could be disproved. There was no evidence of any Aryan people having lived in Sweden much before the time when Persia invaded Greece, and when the ancient Vedic religion, after a sway of many centuries, after long periods of growth and decay, was already being supplanted by a new religion, by Buddhism. The statement quoted as having been made by a defender of the Scandinavian theory, that the date of the Aryan migration into India was about the seventh century, must clearly rest on a misprint, and was probably meant for the seventeenth century. For, after all, whenever the Aryans started from Scandinavia, they must have been near the Indus about 1500 B. C., speaking Vedic, and not modern Buddhist Sanskrit; they must have been in Greece about 1000 B. C., speaking the Dorian dialect of the Greek branch of the Aryan stock of speech. They must have been in Asia Minor, speaking the Ionian dialect of the same Greek branch at a time early enough for their name of *Yavan* to be quoted by the author of Genesis, for their name of *Yauna* to be joined with those of Media and Armenia as provinces of Persia in the cuneiform inscriptions of Darius; nay, possibly for the same name, under the disguise of *Uinen*, being found in Egypt in the hieroglyphic inscriptions of the fifteenth century B. C.

These are facts that have to be accommodated, when we are asked to believe that the ancestors of all these Âryas came from Sweden, where we know of no traces of human life, much less of Aryan life, much before these very wars between Persians and Ionians. Even then we only find *kitchen-middens* and funeral barrows, and who is to tell us whether these *beaux restes* of prehistoric dinners were left by Âryas or by pre-Aryan hordes, and whether these silent dolichocephalic skulls spoke once an Aryan or non-Aryan dialect?

With all these palpable facts against them it can hardly be supposed that the supporters of the Scandinavian theory had no arguments at all on their side. Yes, they had, but let us see what their strength really is.

It has been said that Latham, who first started this theory, pointed out that at present the number of Âryas, speaking different Aryan dialects in Europe, is much larger than the number of Âryas in Asia, and that it would therefore be absurd to derive the majority from so small a minority. First of all, I doubt these linguistic statistics, even at the present day. I am not at all certain that the number of people speaking Aryan dialects in Asia at the present moment is smaller than that of Aryan speakers in Europe. But at the time of which we are now speaking, say 500 B. C., when one great period of language, literature, and religion had already come to an end in India, the population of the North of Europe and of Scandinavia was of the scantiest, and even if they were Âryas, and not Basks, or Laps, or Fins, their number would have been a mere nothing compared with the enormous number of Âryas at that time living in India, and Persia, and Asia Minor. How then these Âryas who composed their Vedic hymns on the banks of the Seven Rivers between 1500 and 1000 B. C., should have migrated from Sweden, passes my understanding.

A stronger argument that has been adduced in favor of Sweden being the cradle of the Aryan race, is a passage from Jordanes, or Jornandes, as he is commonly called. At all events we have here something tangible that can be handled, that can be proved or disproved. It is said that Jordanes has preserved the ancient tradition that Sweden was "the manufactory of people," the *officina gentium*, as he expressed it.

Before we quote an authority, our first duty is to find out who he was and what means of knowledge he possessed. Now Jordanes lived about 550 A. D. He was originally a notary in Bulgaria, and became afterwards a monk, possibly in Ravenna. He wrote a book *De rebus Geticis et De origine actuque Geticae gentis*, which is chiefly based on a lost work of Cassiodorus, the friend and adviser of Theodoric, on Orosius, and on similar authorities. He himself is a most ignorant and uncritical writer. Besides that, he writes with an object, namely to magnify the Gothic race and bring it somehow in connexion with Troy and the fabulous ancestors of the Romans.[1] He certainly, whether rightly or wrongly, believed that the Gothic and other German tribes among whom he had lived on the Danube, came from the north, and from Sweden. He therefore called the island of *Scancia* or

[1] Jordanes, Cap. 9, and 20.

Scandza the *officina gentium*,[1] the manufactory of peoples. But by these peoples he clearly understood the Teutonic tribes, who had overrun the Roman Empire. The idea that other nations, such as Romans, or Greeks, or other Âryas could have come from Sweden would probably have completely staggered his weak mind.

On such evidence then we are asked to believe that tradition had preserved in the year 550 A. D. some recollection of the original migration of the Âryas from Sweden, say 500 B. C. Poor Jordanes himself never dreamt of this, and a theory must indeed be very near drowning to grasp at such a straw.

What would the upholders of the Scandinavian theory say, if *we* appealed to the famous legend of Odin's migration from Asia in support of the Asiatic origin of the Âryas in Europe? And yet that legend meets us only a century later than Jordanes, namely, in Fredegar, 650 A. D., and then grows from century to century till we find it fully developed in the Heimskringla and the Prose Edda in the thirteenth century, nay, believed in by certain scholars of the present day.

If we reason soberly, all we can say is that the separation between the South-Eastern branch of the Aryan family, the Hindus and Persians, and the North-Western branch, the Germans, Celts, Slavs, Greeks, and Italians, cannot be proved to have taken place in Europe, because at that early time we know absolutely nothing of Europe being inhabitable or inhabited by any race, whether Aryan or non-Aryan.

[1] Ex hac igitur Scancia insula, quasi officina gentium, aut certe velut vagina nationum, cum rege suo Berich Gothi quondam memorantur egressi.

The angle from which these two streams of language might have started points to Asia, and points to that very locality where geologists tell us that human life became possible for the first time, the high plateau of Pamir, or rather the valleys sloping down from it towards the South.

We can construct a picture of the life of these as yet undivided Âryas from the words which the Northern and Southern Aryan languages share in common, and all the salient features of that picture fit in with the picture which recent travellers have given us of the neighborhood of Pamir. Let us examine a few of them.

We are told that the climate is cold, the winter long, and that there is plenty of ice and snow. We should therefore expect that the Âryas, before they left that neighborhood, should have formed names for snow and winter, and that these names should have been preserved in both branches of the Aryan family. And so it is. We find in Sanskrit the same words for *snow* and *winter* as in Greek, Latin, and German. This proves at all events that the original home of the Aryan language could not have been in a tropical climate, for there snow and ice being unknown, names for snow and ice would not be wanted.

Snow is *snizh* in ancient Persian, *snaivs* in German, *nix* in Latin. Winter was héman in Sanskrit, *χεῖμα* in Greek, *hiems* in Latin, *zima* in Slavonic. *Ice* is isi in Zend, *îs* in Old High-German.

The most common trees in Northern Kohistân are the pine, the birch, and the oak. One of these trees, the birch, has the same name in Sanskrit and in English. *Birch* in English is bhûr*g*a in Sanskrit. The names of the other trees exist in the South and the

North, and must therefore have been known before the Aryan separation; but their meaning varies. The word which in Sanskrit is used for tree and wood in general, dru, appears in Greek as δρῦς, meaning tree, but especially the oak. In German *triu* is likewise used for tree in general, but in Celtic *daur* means the oak, while in Lituanian *dervà* has become the special name for fir. We see a similar change of meanings in another name for *oak*, the Latin *quercus*. The same word appears in Lombardian as *fereha*, and in the A. S. *furh*, the English *fir*. The *beech* has not a common name in Sanskrit and Greek, whatever the defenders of the Scandinavian theory may say to the contrary. They mistook the name of the birch for that of the beech, and, more than that, they assigned a wrong *habitat* to the beech.

One of the strongest, if not the strongest argument against the Asiatic origin of the Âryas has always been that there are no common Aryan names for lion, and tiger, and camel in their ancient language, while there are common names for swine, sheep, ox, dog, and horse. First of all, this reasoning is not correct. We may safely conclude, when we find the same words in Sanskrit on one side and in Greek and Latin on the other, that these words existed before these languages separated, and that therefore the objects signified were known. But we cannot conclude with the same safety that because the same words do *not* exist in these languages, therefore the objects signified by them could not have been known. Words are constantly lost and replaced. It does not follow, for instance, that the Âryas, before they separated, were ignorant of the use of fire, because the Sanskrit word for fire, agni, is not to be found in Greek. It is replaced in Greek by *πῦρ*, but in Latin the Sanskrit word for fire, agni, appears as *ignis*. Though the positive argument is irresistible, the negative argument has always to be used with great caution. But the latest traveller in Kohistân, M. de Ujfalvy,[1] tells us that even the zoölogical foundation of this argument about lion and tiger is wrong, and that these wild beasts are not to be found in those cold regions where the home of the Âryas is most likely to have been. The fact therefore that the Southern and Northern Aryan languages have not the same names for lion and tiger, so far from being against us, is in perfect harmony with the theory that the original home of the Âryas was on the slopes of the mountains which form the junction between the Hindukush and the Karakorum chains, what may be called Northern Kohistân.

I call it a theory, for I do not see how it can ever be more than a theory. It was in order to guard against useless controversy that I have always confined myself to the statement that the Aryan home was "somewhere in Asia." This has been called a vague and unsatisfactory conclusion;[2] but all who are familiar with these studies know perfectly well what it meant. No one would suspect me of deriving the Âryas from India, Persia, or Asia Minor, nor from Burma, Siam, China, Mongolia, and Siberia, nor from Arabia, Babylon, Assyria, or Phenicia. Then what remains? Not much more than that high plateau from which the Himâlaya chain branches off toward

[1] *Expédition scientifique Francaise en Russie, Sibérie et Turkistan*, par Ch. E. D. Ujfalvy de Mező-Kovesd, Paris, 1878.

[2] See Horatio Hale, "The Aryans in Science and History," in *The Popular Science Monthly*, for March, 1889, p. 673.

the south-east, the Kuen-lün chain towards the east, the Karakorum towards the west, and the Hindukush towards the south-west: the region drained by the feeders of the Indus, the Oxus, and Yaxartes. That is still a sufficiently wide area to accommodate the ancestors of our Aryan race, particularly if we remember in how short a time the offspring of one single pair may grow into millions.

This question has now been so fully discussed, and so splendidly summed up by a Dutch scholar, a Jesuit, worthy of the name and fame which that order once possessed in literature and science, Van den Gheyn,[1] that I hope we shall hear no more of Sweden as the cradle of the Âryas. It would be best, perhaps, to accept a proposal made in the interest of peace by my learned friend and fellow-worker, Professor Sayce, who thinks that he might be able to persuade all ethnologists to use the name *Aryan* in a purely physiological sense, and to restrict it to the dolichocephalic people, with blue eyes and blonde hair, regardless of the language they speak. Whether all people with blue eyes and golden hair in Greece and Italy, in the Caucasus, in Persia, and in Central Asia, have come from Scandinavia, ethnologists would then have to settle among themselves; but we should at all events have peace within our borders. Aryan is a mere adjective, which we could well spare. We should then retain the old classical name of Ârya for those people who brought the numerous varieties of Aryan speech from Asia to Europe, whose thought still runs in our thoughts, as their blood may run in our veins—our true ancestors in spirit and in truth, whether their heads were long, their eyes blue, and their hair golden,

[1] *L'Origine européenne des Aryas*, Paris. 1889.

or whether their heads were round, their eyes dark, and their hair black.

And here I must conclude my plea for the Study of the Science of Language. I hope I have shown you that it really is a disgrace for any human being to go through life without some knowledge of what language is and what it has done for us. There are certain things which are essential to education—not only reading, writing, and arithmetic, but a general knowledge of the earth on which we live (*Geology* and *Geography*); of the sky and the stars which tells us of infinite law and order above (*Astronomy*); of the great men who have made the world what we found it (*History*); and of some of the greatest men who have told us what this world ought to be (*Religion* and *Philosophy*). I add to these the Science of Language which, better than anything else, teaches us what we really are. You have only to try to imagine what this world would be, if it were inhabited by speechless beings, in order to appreciate the full importance of knowing what language really is to us, and how much we owe to language in all we think, and speak, and do.

It is quite true that life is too short for any human being to gain a thorough knowledge of these fundamental subjects. But life is not too short to allow us to gain a sound knowledge of the general outline of these subjects, and of the results that have been garnered up in some of our best school-books and manuals. And this is particularly true with regard to the Science of Language. As I said in a former lecture, we all can play at least one language, many in these days even know two or three. We therefore possess the facts; we have only to digest, to classify, and to try to understand them.

THE STUDY OF SANSKRIT.

It has often been said that no one can know anything of the Science of Language who does not know Sanskrit, and that that is enough to frighten anybody away from its study. But, first of all, to learn Sanskrit in these days is not more difficult than to learn Greek or Latin. Secondly, though a knowledge of Sanskrit may be essential to every student who wishes to do independent work, and really to advance the Science of Language, it is not so for those who simply wish to learn what has been hitherto discovered. It was necessary for those who laid the foundations of our Science to study as many languages as possible, in order to find out their general relationship. Men like Bopp and Pott had to acquire some knowledge of Sanskrit, Zend, Gothic, Lituanian, Old Slavonic, Celtic, Armenian, Georgian, Ossetian, Hebrew, Arabic, and Ethiopian, to say nothing of languages outside the pale of the Aryan and the Semitic families. Their work in consequence was often rough, and it could hardly have been otherwise. When that rough work had been done, it was easy enough to proceed to more minute and special work. But it seems unfair, if not absurd, to find faults with pioneers like Bopp and Pott, because some of their views have been proved to be mistaken, or because they exaggerated the importance of Sanskrit for a successful study of Comparative Philology. Without Sanskrit we should never have had a Science of Language; that seems admitted even by the extreme Left. After the study of Sanskrit had once led to the discovery of a new world, it was but natural that the land should be divided and sub-divided, and that each scholar should cultivate his own special field. Thus Grimm chose the German languages for his special domain, Micklosich the Slavonic, Zeuss the Celtic, Curtius Greek, Corssen Latin. There came, in fact, a reaction, and we were told at last that Sanskrit had nothing more to teach us. Not long ago Manchester, which has taken the lead in so many important movements, informed the world through the *Times* that the long-planned revolution had at last been successful, that Sanskrit was dethroned, that its ministers had been guillotined, and a new claimant had been installed, who had been in hiding in Finland. The Aryan language was a mere bastard of Finnish! However, when the real sources of this information had been discovered, the panic soon came to an end, and scholars worked on quietly as before, each in his own smaller or larger field, unconcerned about the *pronunciamentos* of the Manchester or any other new school. If the rebellion meant no more than that Sanskrit had been shown to be the elder sister only, and not the mother of the other Aryan languages, then I am afraid that I myself must be counted among the oldest rebels. If it meant that the students of Comparative Philology could henceforth dispense altogether with a knowledge of Sanskrit, then I feel sure that by this time the mistake has been found out, and Sanskrit has been restored to its legitimate throne, as *prima inter pares* among the members of the Aryan republic.

It used to be said for a time that even the A B C of Sanskrit was extremely deficient and misleading, and that the system of the Aryan vowels in particular was far more perfect in Greek and German than in

Sanskrit. Sanskrit, we were told, has written signs for the three short vowels only, *ă*, *ĭ*, *ŭ*, not for short *ĕ* and *ŏ*. It was declared to be a very great blemish that the two vowels *ĕ* and *ŏ*, which existed in the primitive Aryan speech, had been lost in Sanskrit. If, however, they were lost in Sanskrit, that, according to the laws of logic, would seem to show that Sanskrit also formerly possessed them, and possibly found that it could do without them. The same spirit of a wise economy may be observed in the historical progress of every language.

But it has now been recognised that, from a grammatical point of view, the Sanskrit system of vowels is really far more true than that of Greek, German, or any other Aryan language. It seems to me altogether wrong, whatever the highest authorities may say to the contrary, to maintain that the Aryan languages began with five, and not with four short vowels.

The Aryan languages possessed from the beginning no more than the well-known four fundamental vowels, namely *i*, *u*, the invariable *a*, and the variable vowel, which changes between *ε*, *o*, and rarely *α*. There are ever so many roots which differ from each other by having either *a*, *i*, *u*, or that fourth variable sound; there are no roots that differ in meaning by having either *α*, *ε*, or *o* as their radical. Hence (*α*) *ε*, *o* represent one fundamental vowel only; they are grammatical variations of one common type.[1]

If we represent roots, as in Hebrew, by their consonants only, then we have in the Aryan languages a root consisting of D and H. With the radical vowel *i*, that root DIH means to knead, with the radical vowel *u* the root DUH means to milk. With the

[1] I use *a* for the invariable a; *α*, *ε*, *o*, for the variable vowel.

third or variable vowel, the root DαH means to burn, and it may appear in certain grammatical derivations as DαH, DεH, or DoH. We never find a root DαH by the side of a root DεH, or a root DεH by the side of the root DoH. What we find, and what has not yet been explained, is that certain roots show a decided predilection for ε or for *o*.

Here then we see how right Sanskrit grammarians were in admitting only four, and not five fundamental vowels, though it might have been better if they had in writing also distinguished between the invariable *a* of A*G*, and the variable α of BHαR. Whether the variable vowel was in Sanskrit also pronounced differently in different grammatical forms, we cannot tell, because in Sanskrit that variable vowel in the body of a word is never written. There are indications, however, in the changes produced in preceding consonants, which seem to speak in favor of such a view.

And nowhere has the importance of a knowledge of Sanskrit been shown more clearly than in the explanation of these very vowel-changes, in Greek and German. Why the variable vowel appears as α, ε, *o* or disappears altogether, why the second and third radical vowels are weakened or strengthened in the same way, remained a perfect mystery, till the key was found in the system of accentuation, preserved in the Vedic Sanskrit, and nowhere else.[1]

But although in this, as in many other cases, Sanskrit betrays more of the ancient secrets of language than Greek or Latin or German, there is plenty

[1] Udâtta in Sanskrit means high, anudâtta not-high. Originally the udâtta syllable represented what we now call *Hochstufe*, the anudâtta *Tiefstufe*, at least during the period when accent meant as yet musical pitch only.

of work, and most important work, to be done in every language, nay in every dialect, for which we want no direct aid from Sanskrit. Some of the most brilliant discoveries in the Science of Language have lately been made by students of Teutonic philology. The work begun in that sphere by Grimm and Scherer has been carried on without any flagging by Fick, Schmidt, Sievers, Osthoff, Collitz, Brugmann and others in Germany, by De Saussure in France, by Ascoli and Merlo in Italy. The same work has been taken up with renewed ardor in England, where Ellis, Morris, Sweet, Skeat, Napier, Douse, and others have done most excellent work, and made valuable additions to our inherited stock of knowledge.

Many more laborers, however, are wanted to cultivate this field of English scholarship. Thousands, as you know, have come forward to gather honey and bring it into the beehive at Oxford, where a Dictionary of the English Language is prepared which, when finished, need not fear comparison with the dictionaries of either Grimm or Littré. But there is much more work to be done in which other thousands might help, such as collecting spoken dialects, watching local pronunciation, gathering old proverbs, writing down with phonetic accuracy popular stories and poems, as repeated by old grannies and young children. If among some of my hearers to-day I have succeeded in raising an interest in language in general, and in kindling a love for their own language in particular, and if that interest and love will bear fruit, however small,—but nothing is too small in the eyes of a conscientious scholar,—then I shall feel amply rewarded for having stayed here to attend your Meeting, which, I hope, may henceforth become a permanent institution in the educational system of our country.

GENEALOGICAL TABLE

OF

THE ARYAN FAMILY OF LANGUAGES.

Living Languages	Dead Languages	Branches	Classes	Division
Spoken Dialects of:—				
India Afghanistân, Pushtu the Gipsies	Modern Sanskrit—Prâkrit and Pâli, Vedic Sanskrit		Indic	South-Eastern Division
Persia Kurdistân Baluchistân Ossethi	Parsi, Pehlevi, Achaemenian Inscriptions, Zend		Iranic	South-Eastern Division
Armenia	Old Armenian			
Wales Brittany +	Old Welsh Old Armorican Cornish	Cymric	Celtic	North-Western Division
Scotland Ireland Isle of Man	Old Irish	Goidelic	Celtic	North-Western Division
+	Inscriptions in Gaul	Gallic	Celtic	North-Western Division
Portugal Spain Provence France Italy Rumania Grisons	Langue d'Oc, Langue d'Oïl | Lingua vulgaris { Oscan, Latin, Umbrian		Italic	North-Western Division
Albania			Illyric	North-Western Division
Greece	Κοινή { Doric, Aeolic; Attic, Ionic		Hellenic	North-Western Division
Lituania + Kurland and Livonia (Lettish)	Old Prussian	Lettic	Windic or Letto Slavic	North-Western Division
Bulgaria Russia (Great, Little, White Russian) Illyria (Slovenian or Carintian, Servian, Croatian)	Ecclesiastical Slavonic	South-East Slavonic	Windic or Letto Slavic	North-Western Division
Poland Bohemia (Slovakian) Lusatia (Wends and Sorbs)	Old Bohemian	West Slavonic	Windic or Letto Slavic	North-Western Division
+	Polabian	West Slavonic	Windic or Letto Slavic	North-Western Division
Germany	Middle and Old High-German	High-German	Teutonic	North-Western Division
+	Gothic		Teutonic	North-Western Division
England Holland Friesland North of Germany (Platt-Deutsch)	Anglo-Saxon Middle and Old Dutch (Low-Franconian) Old Frisian Old Saxon	Low-German	Teutonic	North-Western Division
Denmark Norway Iceland Sweden		Scandinavian	Teutonic	North-Western Division

MY PREDECESSORS.[1]

IN writing my book, *On the Science of Thought*,[2] my chief object was to collect all the facts which seemed to me to bear on the identity of language and thought. I sifted them, and tried to show in what direction their evidence pointed. But, as I imagined myself as addressing a very small special jury, it seemed to me unnecessary, and almost disrespectful, to bring any pressure to bear on them, except the pressure inherent in facts. I therefore did not avail myself as fully as I might otherwise have done, of the many witnesses that I could have brought into court to support by their authority the truth of the theory which I propounded. I mentioned, indeed, their names, but I did not call upon them to speak for me or for themselves. The fact is, that I did not expect that public opinion at large could, at the present moment, be very much interested in a question which had been discussed many times before, but which, as far as I could see, was by nearly all living philosophers,

[1] Reprinted with the consent of publishers and author from the *Contemporary Review*, Vol. LIV.

[2] *The Science of Thought*, Longmans & Co., 1887. *Three Introductory Lectures on the Science of Thought*, delivered at the Royal Institution, with an Appendix, which contains a Correspondence on "Thought Without Words,' between F. Max Müller, Francis Galton, the Duke of Argyll, George J. Romanes, and others. The Open Court Pub. Co., Chicago, Ill., and Longmans & Co., London, 1888.

particularly by those in this country, answered in a direction diametrically opposed to that which I, following the lead of the greatest philosophers of antiquity, of the middle ages, and of more modern times, considered the right one. I know how long I myself living under the influence of prevailing systems of philosophy, had hesitated to give up the old belief that language is a product of thought; that thought must always come first, language after; that thought is independent of language, and that the Greeks were great bunglers when they called language and thought by one and the same name, *Logos.* A long life, devoted to the study of philology and philosophy, was necessary before I could free myself of the old words —that is, the old thoughts—and cease to treat language as one thing and thought as another. Much astronomical observation was required before people could persuade themselves that their evening star was the same as their morning star,[1] and much linguistic observation will have to be performed before anybody will see clearly that our language is really our thought and our thought our language.

But though I was quite prepared that the verdict of living philosophers would, for the present at least, be adverse to my theory, I was not prepared to find nearly all my critics under the impression that this theory of the identity of thought and language was quite a novel theory, something quite unheard of—in fact, a mere paradox. This showed the same want of historical knowledge and tact which surprised so many philosophers in Germany and France at the time of the first appearance of Darwin's book *On the Origin of Species.* Most of the leading reviews in England

[1] See, however, *Hibbert Lectures*, by Sayce, pp. 258, 264.

seemed to consider the theory of evolution as something quite novel, as a kind of scientific heresy, and they held Darwin personally responsible for it, whether for good or for evil. Darwin himself had at last to protest against this misapprehension, to point out the long succession of the advocates of evolution, from Lucretius to Lamarck and Oken, and to claim for himself what he really cared for, a legitimate place in the historical evolution of the theory of evolution.

In Germany and France the doctrine of the identity of language and thought has at once been recognised as an old friend, as a theory that had almost been battered to pieces in former historical conflicts, but which, like the theory of evolution, might well claim for itself a new hearing on account of the immense accumulation of new material, chiefly due to the study of the Science of Language during the present and the past generations. I myself, so far from pretending to propound a new philosophy, thought it right to point out how some of the greatest philosophers have held to the same theory, though without being able to support it by the important evidence supplied by the study of comparative philology, or to perceive quite clearly all the consequences which must flow from it. It seemed certainly strange that a theory which was, to mention more recent philosophers only, accepted without any misgivings by such men as Herder,[1] Schleiermacher, W. von Humboldt, Schelling, and Hegel, in Germany; by Hobbes, Archbishop Whately, and Mansel, in England; by Abelard, De Bonald, De Maistre, and Taine, in France; and by Rosmini in Italy, should have been treated as a complete novelty, or as a mere philological mare's nest,

[1] *Science of Thought*, pp. 30, 129.

by men who stand in the foremost ranks of philosophers in England. What should we say if our best scientific reviews shrank from the theory of the homogeneity of light, heat, and magnetism as an unheard-of novelty, or as a mere scientific paradox? But such has nevertheless been the attitude of some of the best philosophical journals in England, in discussing, or rather in declining to discuss, the identity of language and thought, which in my *Science of Thought* I tried to support, chiefly by the evidence brought together during the last fifty years by the Science of Language.

It may be useful, therefore, to look back, in order to see what form our problem had assumed before the Science of Language had thrown new light upon it. In France this problem of the identity of language and thought has always remained on the order of the day. The controversy between Nominalism and Realism has left there a far deeper impression than in England, and it has not been forgotten that one of the principal tenets of the Nominalists was that our knowledge of universals consisted entirely in words. It was Condillac (1715–1780) and his school in the last century who gave new life to this old controversy, though his well-known dictum, *Nous ne pensons qu'avec les mots*, went certainly beyond the point which had been reached by the older Nominalists.[1] The question is what he meant by *penser*, and if *penser* meant, as it does according to Condillac, no more than *sentir*, it would not be difficult to prove that not only sensation, but also imagination, can take place without language.

[1] "Qu'est ce au fond que la réalité qu'une idée abstraite et générale a dans notre esprit? Ce n'est qu'un nom . . . Les idées abstraites ne sont donc que des dénominations . . . Si nous n'avions point de dénominations, nous n'aurions point d'idées abstraites, nous n'aurions ni genres ni espèces, nous ne pourrions raisonner sur rien." (Condillac, *Logique*, IIme. partie, Chap. V.)

We must define what we mean by thought before we can understand its identity with language. It was Rousseau (1712–1778) who at once perceived the weak point in Condillac's statement. He saw that, if we used the name of thought for all mental work, we ought to distinguish between at least two kinds of thought, thought in images, and thought in words. As a poet and as a dreamer Rousseau was naturally aware how often we are satisfied with images; that is to say, how often we indulge in mere imagination and call it thinking. And though it is quite true that with us who are so saturated with language there are few images which on closer examination turn out to be really anonymous, yet we cannot deny the possibility of such mental activity, and are bound to admit it, particularly in the earlier periods of the development of the human mind. It is this kind of thought which has been often claimed for animals also.[1] Rousseau therefore remarks very justly, *Lorsque l'imagination s'arrête, l'esprit ne marche qu'à l'aide du discours*, "When imagination stops, the mind does not advance, except by means of language."[2]

But, even supposing that our modern philosophers should treat Condillac and Rousseau as ancient and forgotten worthies, surely they must have heard of

1 De Bonald, *De l'Origine du Langage*, p. 67: "Les brutes, qui éprouvent les mêmes besoins, reçoivent aussi les images des objets que l'instinct de leur conservation les porte à fuir ou à chercher, et n'ont besoin de langage. L'enfant, qui ne parle pas encore, le muet qui ne parlera jamais, se font aussi des images des choses sensibles, et la parole nécessaire pour la vie morale et idéale, ne l'est pas du tout à la vie physique."

2 De Bonald, *loc. cit.*, p. 65, remarks: "Ce qui veut dire qu'on ne peut penser qu'au moyen de paroles, lorsqu'on ne pense pas au moyen d'images.' Haller expressed almost the same idea, when he said: "Ita assuevit anima signis uti, ut mera per signa cogitet ac sonorum vestigia sola omnium rerum repraesentationes animae offerant, rarioribus exemplis exceptis, quando affectus aliquis imaginem ipsam revocat."

Dugald Stewart in Scotland (1753–1828), of De Bonald (1754–1840) and De Maistre (1754–1821) in France. Now, Dugald Stewart was not ashamed to teach what the Nominalists had taught before him—namely, that, for the purpose of thinking three things are necessary: *universalia*, *genera*, and *words*. If Dugald Stewart had not persuaded himself that Sanskrit was a mere forgery of the Brahmans, he might have learned a new lesson —namely, that all our words, even those which we call singular, are derived from general concepts, in so far as they must be traced back to roots embodying general concepts. This discovery, however, was reserved for later comers. In the meantime, men like De Bonald and De Maistre in France did not allow the old argument to sleep. But curiously enough, while formerly the idea of the identity of thought and language was generally defended by philosophers of the type of Hobbes, by the supporters of sensualistic theories who derive all our knowledge from the impressions of the senses and their spontaneous associations, we have in De Bonald and De Maistre men of the very opposite stamp—orthodox, almost mystic philosophers, who nevertheless make the identity of thought and language the watchword of their philosophy. It is true that even Bossuet (1627–1704) inclined in the same direction. In his famous treatise, *De la Connaissance de Dieu et de soi-même*, he allows that we can never, or, with the usual proviso of weak-kneed philosophers, hardly ever, think of anything without its name presenting itself to us. But De Bonald went far beyond this, as will be seen from the following extracts:[1]—

[1] *Œuvres de M. de Bonald, Recherches Philosophiques sur les Premiers Objets des Connaissances Morales.* Paris. 1858.

In his treatise on the origin of language he says: "There was geometry in the world before Newton, and philosophy before Descartes, but before language there was absolutely nothing but bodies and their images, because language is the necessary instrument of every intellectual operation—nay, the means of every moral existence."[1] He puts the same idea into more powerful, though at first sight somewhat perplexing language, when he says: "Man thinks his word before he speaks his thought, or, in other words, man cannot speak his thought without thinking his word."[2]

De Maistre, who belongs to the same school as De Bonald, and whose ultimate conclusions I should feel most unwilling to adopt, shows, nevertheless, the same clear insight into the nature of language. Thus he writes: "The question of the origin of ideas is the same as the question of the origin of language; for thought and language are only two magnificent synonyms. Our intellect cannot think nor know that it thinks without speaking, because it must say, 'I know.'"[3]

And again: "It is absolutely the same thing whether one asks the definition, the essence, or the name of an object![4] . . . In one word, there is no word which does not represent an idea, and which is not really as correct and as true as the idea, because thought and language do not differ essentially, but represent the same act of the mind, speaking either to himself or to others."[5]

1 *Loc. cit.*, p. 73.

2 *Loc. cit.*, p. 64: "L'homme pense sa parole avant de parler sa pensée; ou autrement, l'homme ne peut *parler* sa pensée sans *penser* sa parole."

3 *Soirées de St. Pétersbourg*, I., p. 75.

4 *Loc. cit.*, I., p. 135.

5 *Loc. cit.*, I., p. 131.

I say once more that I am the last person to follow these French philosophers to their last conclusions. Their object is to show that language, being what it is, cannot have been a human invention, but must have been a divine revelation.[1] I quote them here as representative men only, and as showing how familiar the idea of the identity of thought and language was on the Continent during the first half of our century—an idea which, by some of the most prominent philosophers in England, has been treated as an unheard-of paradox.

Of course it may be said that De Bonald, and De Maistre too, are ancient history; that the first half of this century was a mistake, and that true and positive philosophy dates only from the second half of our century. But even then, those who wish to take part in the discussion of the great problems of philosophy ought to know that the question of the identity of language and thought has never to the present day been neglected by the leading philosophers of Germany and France. Let us take one, who has not only proved himself most intimately acquainted with the most recent schools of philosophical thought in England, but has often been claimed as a disciple of Stuart Mill—let us take M. Taine, and what do we find in his great work, *De l'Intelligence*, first published in 1870? Without the slightest hesitation, without any

[1] "Si l'expression est nécessaire, non-seulement à la production de l'idée ou à sa révélation extérieure, mais encore à sa conception dans notre propre esprit; c'est-à-dire, si l'idée ne peut être présenté à notre esprit ni présenté à l'esprit des autres que par la parole orale ou écrite : le langage est *nécessaire*, ou tel que la société n'a pu, dans aucun temps, exister sans le langage, pas plus que l'homme n'a pu exister hors de la société. L'homme n'a donc pas inventé le langage . . . . La nécessité de la révélation primitive du langage a été défendue dans *l'Encyclopédie* par le savant et vertueux Beauzée. Charles Bonnet et Hugh Blair entrent dans le même sentiment."—DE BONALD, *loc. cit.*, p. 199.

fear that what he says could sound strange to well-schooled philosophical ears, or be taken for mere paradox even by the outside public, he writes:[1]—

"What we call a general idea is nothing but a name; not the simple sound which vibrates in the air and sets our ears in motion, nor the assemblage of letters which blacken the paper and touch our eyes—not even these letters apprehended mentally, or the sound of them mentally rehearsed, but that sound and those letters endowed, as we perceive or imagine them, with a twofold character, first of producing in us the images of individuals belonging to a certain class, and of these individuals only; secondly, of reappearing every time when an individual of that class, and only when an individual of that same class, presents itself to our memory or our perception."

And again:[2]—

"Hence arise curious illusions. We believe we possess, besides our general words, general ideas; we distinguish between the idea and the word; the idea seems to us a separate act, the word being an auxiliary only. We actually compare the idea and the image, and we say that the idea performs in another sphere the same office in presenting to us general objects which the image performs in presenting to us individuals . . . Such is the first of our psychological illusions, and what we call our consciousness swarms with them. The false theories arising from them are as complicated as they are numerous. They obstruct all science, and only when they shall have been swept away will science become simple again."

I could go on quoting passage after passage from

[1] *Loc. cit.*, I., p. 35.

[2] *Loc. cit.*, I., p. 66.

M. Taine's work, and I may say, with regard to him too, that, though accepting his facts, I by no means accept all the conclusions he draws from them. I agree with him that word and idea are but two names for the same thing. I agree with him, when he, like Locke, shows the impossibility of animals ever reaching the intellectual level of language, for the simple reason that they cannot reach the level of general ideas. But I differ from him when he thinks that the origin of language and the original formation of words can be explained by watching the way in which a child of the present day acquires the use of a language ready made, though even here our opinions are by no means so far apart as he imagines. We are concerned with different problems, but we agree, at all events, as to the manner in which these problems ought to be treated, not by mere assertion and counter-assertion, but by a comprehensive study of facts, and by a careful examination of the opinions of those who came before us.

The unhistorical treatment of philosophy, for which some English philosophers have been of late frequently, and, I think, justly, reprehended, entails far more serious consequences than might be imagined. I admit it gives a certain freshness and liveliness to philosophical discussions. Completely new ideas, or ideas supposed to be new, excite, no doubt, greater enthusiasm, and likewise greater surprise and indignation. But life, nay, even history, would be too short, if we were always to begin again where Thales, Aristotle, or Descartes began, or if the well-known results of Kant's *Critique of Pure Reason* were published to the world as the most recent discoveries of synthetic philosophy.

Another inconvenience arising from this unhistorical treatment of philosophical questions is felt even more acutely—namely, that in defending an old theory by new arguments we are often supposed to be pleading our own cause. Darwin, particularly in his earlier books, speaks of the cause of evolution, not as if it were anything personal to himself, but as a trust handed down to him, almost as an heirloom of his family; anyhow, as a valuable inheritance dating from the earliest days of awakening physical and philosophical inquiry. In his later books he becomes more and more self-conscious, and seems restrained from applying that rapturous language to the results obtained by the theory of evolution which those who follow him feel perfectly justified in applying to his and their own labors. I have been blamed for speaking with unconcealed rapture of the theory of the identity of language and thought, and I certainly should feel that I deserved blame if this theory had really been of my own invention. But, knowing how many of the most authoritative philosophers had held the same views, I felt at perfect liberty to speak of it, as I did, as the most important philosophical truth, in fact, as the only solid foundation of all philosophy.

I also took it for granted, though it seems I ought not to have done so, that the misunderstandings which had formerly beset this theory, and had been demolished again and again, would not be repeated with the innocent conviction that they had never been thought of before.

Of course, such an expression as identity of thought and language can be cavilled at. If Kant is right, no two things in space and time can ever be identical, and if people really take identical in that sense, the sooner the word is altogether superseded the better. When we say that language and thought are identical, we mean that they are two names of the same thing under two aspects. There is a very useful term in Sanskrit philosophy, "ap*ri*thagbhâva" ("the not being able to exist apart"), and it is this, the impossibility of thought existing apart from language, or language from thought, which we mean when we call the two identical. We can distinguish for our own purposes, and these purposes are perfectly legitimate, between the sound and the meaning of a word, just as we can distinguish between the pitch and the timbre of our voice. But though we can distinguish, we cannot separate the two. We cannot have timbre without pitch, nor pitch without timbre; neither can we have words without thought, nor thought without words. There never was on one side a collection of vocables, mere *flatus vocis*, and on the other a collection of concepts. The two were always one and indivisible, but not one and indistinguishable. We can certainly distinguish the sound of a word from its meaning, but we must not expect to meet with meanings walking about in broad daylight as disembodied ghosts, or with sounds floating through the air, like so many Undines in search of a soul. The two were not two, but were one from the beginning, and the *πρῶτον ψεῦδος* lies in this attempted divorce between sound and meaning.

After words have been formed, as embodied thoughts, no doubt it is possible to imitate and repeat their sound without knowing their meaning. We have only to speak English to a Chinaman, and we shall see that what to us is English is to him mere sound and jabber. It is no longer language, because it is of the essence of language to be sound and meaning at the same time.

But then it is asked—Is our thinking always speaking? I say, yes it is, if only we take speaking in its proper sense. But if we mean by speaking the mere vibrations of our vocal chords, then thinking is not always speaking, because we can suppress these vibrations, and yet keep in our memory the sound which they were meant to produce, and the meaning which that sound was meant to convey. It is this speaking without voice which has come to be called thinking, while thinking aloud has monopolised the name of speaking. The true definition, in fact, of thinking, as commonly understood, is speaking *minus* voice. And as this kind of thinking is that which is most commonly used for intense intellectual work, people have become so proud of it that they cannot bear to see it what they call degraded to mere speaking without voice. Still so it is, as every one can discover for himself, if he will only ask himself at any moment what he is or has been thinking about. He can answer this question to himself and to others in words only. Nor is there anything degrading in this, and, at all events, the greatest philosophical thinkers, the Greeks, did not think so, or say so, for they were satisfied with one and the same word for thought and speech.

Nor do we really, when we examine ourselves carefully, ever detect ourselves as thinking only, or as thinking in the abstract. How often have I been asked, not whether I think without words, but whether I think in English or in German. What does that mean? It means, whether I speak to myself in English or in German, and no more. The idea that I could speak to myself in no language at all is too absurd to be even suggested.

The results which the Science of Language has arrived at, and which are by no means so startling as has been supposed, are shortly these:—We have sensations without language, and some of these sensations may produce in men, as well as in animals, involuntary cries.

We have perceptions, or images without language, and some of these may be accompanied by gestures or signs, such gestures or signs being often intelligible to others belonging to the same kind.

We have concepts, but these we can never have without words, because it is the word which embodies originally one feature only of the whole image, and afterwards others, and thus supplies what we call abstract concepts, to which nothing can ever respond in imagination, nothing in sensation, nothing in nature.

Here it is where the Science of Language has supplied the historical proof of what would otherwise have remained a mere postulate. We know, as a fact, that about eight hundred roots will account for nearly the whole wealth of the Sanskrit Dictionary. We can account for these roots in different ways, the most unobjectionable being that suggested by Noiré, that they were originally the *clamor concomitans* of the conscious acts of men. Now, let us take an instance. Man would have received the sensation of brightness from the stars in the sky, and it is possible, at least I should not like to deny it, that animals too might receive the same sensation. After a time, when the same starry sky was observed night after night, and year after year, the stars as bright points would be remembered, and would leave an image of separate sparkling points, nay, it may be, of certain very prominent constellations in our memory. Nor is there any reason to doubt that, without any language, the mere image of certain constellations appearing on the sky might from the earliest times have evoked the images of concomitant events, such as the approach of cold weather, or the return of spring, in the minds of our most savage ancestors.

But with all that, there was as yet no word, and, in consequence, no concept of a star. What we call stars, as different from the sky to which they seem attached, as different also from sun and moon, were as yet bright images only.

Now, the next decisive step was this. The Aryan man possessed what we call roots, sounds which had often been used while he and his friends were engaged in acts of scattering, dispersing, strewing. One of these sounds may have been STAR. We find it in Latin, *ster-no* and *stramen*; in Greek, *στορ-έννυμι*; in Gothic, *strauja*; English, to *strew*, and its many derivatives, In all these words, the root, we say, is STAR, though we need not assert that such a root ever existed by itself before it was realised in all the words which sprang from it. One of the features of the bright sparkling points in heaven was their scattering or strewing sprays of light. By means of the root STAR this one feature was abstracted from the rest of the image, and the stars were thus at the same time called and conceived as strewers: in Sanskrit, *star-as*; in Greek, *ἀστέρ-ες*; in Latin, *stellae*, i. e. *sterulae*; in English, *stars*.

This word *star* was not meant for any single star, it did not correspond to a sensation, nor to any vague image or recollection of stars; it was a name representing one abstract feature of the stars, namely, their scattering of light in a dark night. It was man's own creation, and corresponded to nothing in nature, unless it was predicated afterwards of this or that particular star. It was so general, in fact, that, as soon as special stars had to be named, new determining or individualising names became necessary. When it was observed that certain stars always retained their place, while others travelled about, the former were named fixed stars, the latter travellers or planets,[1] till at last every prominent star received some kind of name, that is to say, was known and called as different from all the rest.

We see the same process everywhere, though it is not always possible to discover with perfect certainty what specific features in the objects of nature were selected for the purpose of knowing and naming them, or, in other words, from what root their names were derived. Let us examine the name of *tree*. Here it is quite clear that the most primitive savage must have had the sensation produced by trees growing up all around him, and giving him shelter against the sun, possibly supplying food also to appease his hunger. Let us suppose that that sensation was on a level with the sensation which animals also receive from trees. I do not think it was, but I am willing to grant it for argument's sake. The hundreds and thousands of trees which made an impression on the eyes of these savages must soon have become indistinguishable, and left an image in the memory of a very general and indistinct character. Some philosophers maintain that animals also have these blurred images, and that they

[1] *Lectures on the Science of Language*, I., p. 8.

would mistake a post for a tree. Again, for argument's sake, I do not mean to contest it.

But now comes a new step. Men, and men alone, in the earliest stages of their life on earth, began to take hold of certain trees, tear off their bark, hollow out their stems, and use these in the end for making beds, boats, and tables, and for other purposes. Concomitant and significative of this act of tearing off the bark of trees, the Aryan people had a root DAR; in Greek, *δείρω*; in English, *to tear*. Being chiefly interested in trees because they could thus be peeled and shaped and rendered useful, they called a tree in Sanskrit *dru*; in Greek, *δρῦς*; in Gothic, *triu*; in English, *tree*. This was but one out of many names that could be applied to trees for various reasons, more or less important in the eyes of the Aryan savages; and here, even for the sake of argument, I cannot bring myself to admit that any animal could have done the same. We must bear in mind that there is really nothing in nature corresponding to tree. If it simply meant what could be shaped, there are hundreds of things that can in various ways be shaped. If it was confined to trees, there are again hundreds of trees, oaks, beeches, fir-trees, etc.; but no human eye has ever seen a tree, nor could any artist give us an idea of what a tree may be as a mere phantasma in the mind of man or animal.[1]

If all this is true, it follows that no concept, not even the concept of so simple an object as a tree, was possible without a name. It was by being named, that is, by having one of its prominent features singled out or abstracted, and brought under the root DAR, to tear, that the blurred image, left on the mem-

[1]Taine, *De l'Intelligence*, I., p. 27.

ory after repeated sensations, became known, became definite, received a handle for the purposes of thought and speech. And what was the result? The result was that with the name there arose in the mind, not a sensation, not an image—for think what such an image would have been—but what we call a concept, when we speak to ourselves without vibrations of the vocal chords, but what is called a word when uttered aloud. If we distinguish, therefore, at all between concepts and words, we are bound to say that concepts are due to words, they are words *minus* sound, and not, as most philosophers will have it, that words are due to concepts, that they are concepts *plus* sound. It is only because to think aloud is to speak that to speak *sotto voce* may be called to think. All this was perfectly known, as far as the general principle is concerned. I believe that even Berkeley's ingenious views of general ideas might easily be translated into our language. He maintains that general ideas do not exist at all; so do we. He then proceeds to say that what we call general ideas are particular ideas with a word attached to them. So do we,[1] only that we have learned how this process took place. It could not be done by taking a sound at random and attaching it to a particular idea, for the simple reason that there were no such sounds in the market. But if Berkeley had known the results of the Science of Language, he would, I believe, have been perfectly satisfied with the process, as described before, of bringing one feature of the particular idea under a root, and thus raising that particular into a general idea at the same time that the root was raised into a word.

We could come to an understanding with Locke

[1] *Science of Thought*, p. 259.

also, when he says that "words become general by being made the signs of general ideas!"[1] if only he could be made to see that the same object which he has in view can be attained by saying that ideas become general by being signed with a word.

Nor should I despair of establishing a perfect agreement with M. Taine, if only he would leave the modern Parisian nursery and follow me into the distant caves of our Aryan ancestors. Nothing can be more brilliant than the way in which he describes the process of generalisation going on in the mind of a child.[2] He describes how the nurse, on showing a dog to a child, says *oua-oua*, how the child's eyes follow the nurse's gestures, how he sees the dog, hears his bark, and how, after a few repetitions which form his apprenticeship, the two images, that of the dog and that of the sound, become, according to the law of the association of images, associated permanently in his mind. Thus, when he sees the dog again, he imagines the same sound, and by a kind of imitative instinct he tries to utter the same sound. When the dog barks, the child laughs and is enchanted, and he feels all the more tempted to pronounce the sound of the animal, which strikes him as new, and of which he had hitherto heard a human imitation only. Up to this point there is nothing original or superior; the brain of every mammal is capable of similar associations. What is peculiar to man is that the sound associated by him with the perception of a certain individual is called forth again, not only by the sight of exactly similar individuals, but likewise by the presence of distinctly different individuals, though with

[1] *Loc. cit.*, p. 259.

[2] *Loc. cit.*, p. 245.

regard to certain features belonging to the same class. In fact, analogies which do not strike an animal, strike man. The child says *oua-oua* at the sight of the dog belonging to the house. Soon he says *oua-oua* at the sight of poodles, pugs, and Newfoundland dogs. A little later the child will say *oua-oua* to a toy dog which is made to bark by some kind of mechanism, and this no animal would do. Even a toy dog which does not bark, but moves on wheels—nay, a dog made of bronze, standing motionless and dumb in the drawing-room, a small friend walking on all fours in the nursery, lastly a mere drawing, will evoke the same sound.

All this is true, perfectly true; and M. Taine may be quite right in maintaining that the discoveries of Oken, Goethe, and Newton are in the end due to the same power of discovering analogies in nature. I follow him even when he sums up in the following words:—

> "To discover relations between most distant objects, to disentangle most delicate analogies, to establish common features in the most dissimilar things, to isolate most abstract qualities, all these expressions have the same meaning, and all these operations can be traced back to the name being evoked by perceptions and representations possessing the slightest resemblances, to the signal being roused by an almost imperceptible stimulant, to the mental word appearing in court at the first summons."

With certain restrictions, all these observations made among children of the present day apply with equal force to the children of our race.[1] When, for instance, such a word as *dru*, tree, had once been formed, supposing that at first it was meant for such

[1] See also L. M. Billia, *Due Risposte al Prof. Angelo Valdarnini intorno a una pretesa contraddizione fra la dottrina ideologica e la psicologica del Rosmini.* Torino, 1887, p. 14.

trees only as could be peeled and smoothed and fashioned into some useful tools, it would soon be transferred to all trees, whatever their wood. After that, it might become specialised again, as we see in Greek, where δρῦς means chiefly oak, and in Lithuanian, where it means pine.[1] On the other hand, we see a word such as *oak*, after it had taken its definite meaning, becoming generalised again, and being used in Icelandic for trees in general.

With regard to all this I see no difference between M. Taine's views and my own, and I likewise fully agree with him, when he explains how in the end every word, before it is used for philosophical purposes, has to be carefully defined.[2]

There is, however, some new and important light which the Science of Language has thrown on this old problem, and which, if M. Taine had taken it into account, would have enabled him, not only to establish his own views more firmly, but to extend them far beyond the narrow walls of our modern nurseries. The Science of Language has clearly shown that every word coincides from the very beginning with a general concept. While formerly the admission that thought was impossible without words was mostly restricted to general and abstract terms, we can now extend it to singular terms likewise, in fact, to the whole of our language, with the exception of interjections and what are called demonstrative elements. That no one could think whiteness, goodness, or even humanity or brutality was generally admitted, even by those who hesitated to admit that no thought was possible without language. But now that we can prove historically

[1] *Loc. cit.*, I., pp. 39, 57.

[2] *Biographies of Words*, p. 258.

that even a tree could not have been named except as coming under the general term of tearing, peeling, shaping, or, in other cases, of feeding, sheltering, or growing, no wavering or haggling is any longer possible. All our words are conceptual, all our concepts are verbal : this is what Nominalism postulated without being able to prove it, that is what Nominalism has proved by means of the discoveries which a comparative study of languages has placed at our disposal, and which no scepticism can touch. From the first, Comparative Philology had no such ulterior objects in view. It confined itself to a careful collection of facts, to the analysis of all that had become purely formal, to the discovery of the constituent elements of language, to the establishment of the genealogical relationship of all members of the same family of speech ; but beyond this it did not mean to go. When, however, some of the results at which Comparative Philology had arrived quite independently, were found to be almost identical with the teachings of some of the most authoritative philosophers ; when it was found, for instance, that while Locke maintained that animals had no general ideas because they had no words, the Science of Language had arrived at the conclusion that animals had no words because they had no general ideas,[1] the Science of Language became *ipso facto* the Science of Thought, and language and thought were recognised once more as two faces of the same head.

The consequences which follow by necessity from this recognition of the identity of thought and language, and which I was anxious to put forward as strongly as possible in my *Science of Thought*, may, no doubt, have startled some philosophers whose chief

[1] *Lectures on the Science of Language*, I., p. 65.

strength lies in the undefined use of words. But that theory itself could never have startled a careful student of the history of philosophy. It is a very old friend with a new face, and had a right to expect a different reception.

To the Greeks, we know, it was so natural to look upon language and thought as two sides of the same thing, that we can hardly appeal to them as conscious upholders of such a theory. As they used *logos* in both senses, as discourse, whether internal or external, their knowledge of the identity of language and thought came to them by intuition rather than by reflexion. They had never been led astray as we have been; hence they had not to discover the right way.

Still, whenever Greek philosophers come to touch on this question, they speak with no uncertain tone, though even then they are generally satisfied with stating the truth, without attempting to prove what, in their eyes, seemed hardly to require any proof—namely, the identity of language and thought.

In the *Sophist*, Plato begins by showing how language (λόγος) may be true or false, and only after having proved this, does he proceed to show that thought and imagination also may be true or false. For, he proceeds, "thought (διάνοια) is the same as language, with this exception, that thought is the conversation of the soul with herself which takes place without voice, while the stream which, accompanied by sound, flows from thought through the lips, is called language (λόγος)." He then defines opinion (δόξα) as the result of thinking (διανοίας ἀποτελεύτησις), and imagination (φαντασία) as the union of opinion and sensation. In this way only, that is, by proving that thought, opinion, and imagination are closely akin to language, does he establish in the end that, as language has been proved to be either true or false, thought, opinion, and imagination also may be true or false.

Whether Plato could not have established the possibility of truth and falsehood in thought, opinion, and imagination by a simpler and shorter process, is not the question which concerns us here. What concerns us is the perfect assurance with which he identifies here, as well as in the *Theaetetus* (190),[1] speech (λόγος) and thought (διάνοια), an assurance which seems to be shared by his latest translator, Professor Jowett, when finding fault with Hegel because "he speaks as if thought, instead of being identical with language, was wholly independent of it."[2]

Now, therefore, when it will hardly be safe to say any longer that the identity of language and thought is something quite unheard of, a paradox, a mere perversity (all these expressions have been used by men who call themselves philosophers, and even professors of philosophy), the next step will probably be to treat it as a mere question of words.

And, indeed, it is a question of words, but in the true sense of that word.[3]

If we use *thought* promiscuously for every kind of mental process, it stands to reason that to say that thought is impossible without language would be ab-

1 "What do you mean by thinking?" "I mean by thinking the conversation which the soul holds with herself in thinking of anything. . . . I say, then, that to form an opinion is to speak, and opinion is a word spoken, I mean, to oneself and in silence, not aloud, or to another."

2 *Plato*, Vol. IV., p. 420. Hegel, however, said: "We think in names;" see *Science of Thought*, p. 45.

3 "Ein Wortstreit entsteht daraus, weil ich die Sachen unter andern Kombinationen sentire und drum, ihre Relativität ausdrückend, sie anders benennen muss."—Goethe an Lavater, 1774.

surd. To feel pain and pleasure is an inward mental process, to see and hear are inward mental processes; to stare at the images of present and past events, to build castles in the air, to feed on such stuff as dreams are made of—all this might certainly be brought under the general category of mental activity. For ordinary purposes we need not be too particular about language, and, if people like to call all this *thinking*, why should we object? I, myself, when there can be no misunderstanding, use *thought* in that general sense, and use the word *mind* for all that is going on within us, whether sensation, perception, conception or naming.[1] I did not, therefore, put on my title-page, "No thought without language," but "No reason without language," and I did so after having defined reason as the addition and subtraction of conceptual words.

But though admitting this general meaning of *thinking*, we should carefully distinguish it from its more special and technical use, when it becomes synonymous with reasoning, and is, in fact, speaking *sotto* or *senza voce*. Whenever there is danger of misapprehension, it is decidedly better to avoid it by definition, but in most cases it is quite clear whether to *think* is used in its general or in its special sense. If, therefore, it is said that the question of the identity of thought and language is a mere question of words, I say, Yes, it is; but so is every question of philosophy, if rightly understood. Words are terms, and only if rightly determined do they enable us to reason rightly. Let the word *thought* be rightly defined, and let the word *language* be rightly defined, and their identity will require no further proof; for, when we maintain their identity, we do not mean by language mere sound,

[1] *Science of Thought*, p. 20.

nor do we mean by thought mere sensation or imagination, but knowledge of something that can neither be felt nor imagined, and can only be signified. We can never see nor can we imagine *tree*, *dog*, *man*, *triangle*, *polygon*, *parallelopiped*, and all the rest of our dictionary. Then what are *tree*, *dog*, *man*, and all the rest? They are names (*nomina*=*gnomina*), that is, acts of knowledge, and of that peculiar class of knowledge which cannot possibly have anything corresponding to it in sensuous perception or imagination, because it has always reference to something which we discover in and lift out from percepts in order to signify whole classes of percepts, but never any real and individual percept. We can afterwards use these names, and say, for instance, this is a tree, this is a dog; but *tree* and *dog*, which we thus predicate, are general and abstract terms; they are not *the* fir-tree or *the* poodle dog which our sensation and imagination present to us.

I hope that, after this definition of the true meaning of language and thought, the usual result will follow, and that my critics will say that, if I meant no more than that, no one would think of differing from me, and that I have only myself to blame for not having made my meaning clear. I am quite willing to take that blame so long as I may agree with my adversaries quickly. If people will only see what "a question of words" really means, I believe there will soon be peace among all contending philosophical parties.

But, unfortunately, we think but too much in words, and almost let them think for us, instead of making them completely our own. We take our words as they come to us by inheritance, and we trust that other people will take them in the same sense in which we use them.

And yet nothing is more certain than that two people hardly ever take the same word in the same sense, and that just the most important words are often used in entirely different senses by different philosophers. Hence all our misunderstandings, all our quarrellings, all our so-called systems of philosophy, every one differing from the other, and yet all starting from the same given facts, all collected by the same eyes and the same minds!

If all philosophers used the same words in the same sense, their conclusions would differ as little as the conclusions of mathematicians. A mathematician knows exactly what is the meaning of the terms with which he operates, while philosophers will hardly ever condescend to define the terms which they use. We wonder why mathematicians always arrive at the same results, or, if they do not, why they can always discover the mistakes they have made. But how could it be otherwise? Even their highest problems, which completely stagger the unmathematical mind, consist in the end in nothing but addition and subtraction. Our reasoning also, even when it reaches the highest metaphysical problems, consists in nothing but addition and subtraction. What else could it consist in? But there is this difference, that, while the mathematician adds and subtracts values which are defined within the strictest limits, the philosopher adds and subtracts values which are often not defined at all, or defined within the vaguest limits. If the metaphysician does not actually play with loaded dice, he often uses dice which he has never examined, and which, for all he knows, may have been marked rightly or wrongly by those who placed them in his hands. If all our words were defined as triangles, squares, and spheres are in geometry, or as 1.999 is in arithmetic philosophy would soon become a worthy rival of mathematics.

The only hope of peace and of an understanding between various schools of philosophy lies in definition, and definition ought at the present moment to be the chief employment of all honest philosophers.

But we want more than definition—we want a thorough purification of language. A perfect language ought to be like a perfect alphabet. As in a perfect alphabet the same letter ought always to have one and the same sound, and the same sound ought always to be represented by one and the same letter, so, in a perfect language, the same word ought always to have one and the same meaning, and the same meaning ought always to be represented by one and the same word. I know all poets will cry out against this heresy, but I am speaking of philosophical, not of poetical, language.

Languages suffer from wealth even more than from poverty. The human mind is so made that it is always inclined to presuppose a difference of meaning where there is a difference of names. Because we have a number of names to signify what is going on within us, such as spirit, mind, understanding, intelligence, and reason, philosophers have made every kind of effort to show how each differs from the rest, till we seem to have ever so many pigeon-holes within us, and ever so many pigeons hatching their eggs in them, instead of one undivided mental activity, applied to different objects.

While here confusion is due to too great a wealth of expression, we saw before how the employment of the word *language* in totally different senses, or poverty of expression, played equal havoc with our thoughts. If we can speak of the language of the eyes, of the language of silence, of the language of flowers, of the language of animals, no wonder that we forget altogether the distinctive meaning of language when used in the definite sense of expression of conceptual thought by conceptual words. Let this definition of language be granted, and ever so many books might have remained unwritten. We are all dealing with the same facts when we say that animals have no language, while others say they have language. We may go on forever collecting anecdotes of parrots and jackdaws, we shall never come to a mutual understanding. But let language be once defined, and all wrangling will cease. If language is defined as communication in general, we shall all agree that animals have language. If language means human language, conceptual language, language derived from roots, then we shall all agree that animals have no language.

But it is not only in philosophy that we want a *katharsis* of human speech; it is wanted in every sphere of human thought. Think of the different meanings attached to the word *gentleman*. From the most opposite quarters, from high and low, you hear the expression, "He is a gentleman," or "He is not a gentleman." If you venture to doubt, or are bold enough to ask for a definition of gentleman, you run a considerable risk of being told that you are not a gentleman yourself if you do not know what gentleman means. Yet the butler will call you a gentleman if you give him ten shillings instead of half-a-crown; your friends will doubt whether you are a gentleman if you indulge in that kind of menial generosity. And if there is this haze about the meaning of gentleman, think of the polychromatic iridescence that plays round the name of *lady*. The best we can do when we are asked to define that word is to say that it cannot be defined, and that to define means to destroy its charm, which can be felt only, but cannot be analysed.

If you wish to see a real confusion of tongues, you need not go to the plain in the land of Shinar, but read any article on art in any of our leading reviews. If you were to ask for a definition of almost any word used in these reviews, whether nice, sweet, charming, felicitous, exquisite, lovely, heavenly, or realistic, warm, throbbing, bewitching, killing, and all the rest, you would fare very badly. You would be called a pedant, or an ignoramus, and you would require no definition of what is meant by *these* words.

Look for a moment at political language. An eminent politician has lately spoken in rapturous terms about the name of Home Rule. He called it so delightful a term, so apt, so full of meaning. To others it seems the most stupid word that has lately been invented, and exactly for the same reason—namely, because it is so full, so brimful of meaning. Define Home Rule, and if we do not all of us become Home Rulers at once, we shall at all events be able to compare notes, to arrive at a mutual understanding, and to find out what is practicable and what is not. Every individual, every home, every town, every county has a right to so much individual liberty, to so much Home Rule, to so much municipal freedom, to so much county government, as is compatible with the vital interest of the commonwealth. All individual claims that clash with the welfare of the larger communities must be surrendered, some for a time, others in perpetuity. Home Rule, in its undefined meaning, is certainly brimful of meaning, but these words overflowing with meaning are exactly the most bewildering and the most misleading terms. Home Rule may mean liberty, independence, self-government, and a careful regard to local interests. In that sense we are all Home Rulers. But it may also mean licence, sedition, and selfishness—and in that sense, I hope, the number of Home Rulers is very small in the United Kingdom of Ireland, Scotland, and England.

But much more serious consequences may follow from a careless use of words. Politics, after all, are but a small section of ethics, and we have lately seen a complete sytem of ethics built up on the ambiguous use of the word *good*. No doubt, a knife, or a gun, or a house may be called good, if they are well adapted to cut, to shoot, and to shelter. We may also speak of actions as good or bad, not in a moral sense, but simply as answering their purpose. A shot, for instance, may be called a good shot, if it is well aimed and well delivered, even though it should be the shot of a murderer. The first arrow which William Tell let fly at the apple on the head of his son was a good shot, but there was no moral element in it, because the father acted under constraint. But if he had wounded his son, and then, as he intended, had shot the second arrow at Gessler, that might likewise have been a good shot, in one sense, but, from a moral point of view, it would have been murder.

But to say that moral actions also are called good or bad, according as the adjustments of acts to ends are or are not efficient, is mere jugglery with words. *Good* has two meanings, and these two meanings should be kept carefully apart. Good may mean useful, but good also means what is anything but useful or profitable; and it is goodness in that sense which moral philosophy has to account for. It is quite open to any philosopher to say that nothing should be called good except what is in some sense or other useful. But in that case the meaning of usefulness ought to be properly defined; we ought not to imagine that, because we use the same word, we are thinking the same thought. Now, how does our utilitarian philosopher define moral usefulness? He maintains that as the preservation and prolongation of our own life are our *summum bonum*, any acts conducing to this should be called good. Here many people would question the statement that preservation, and, more particularly, prolongation, of life beyond a certain term could always be called the highest good; but, even admitting this, we might indeed call cannibalism useful, for the preservation and prolongation of life, but we should hardly call it good.

It is different when we come to consider the two other spheres of action in which we are told that any acts useful for the preservation and prolongation of life of our own offspring, and of our fellow creatures, should be called good.

Here we must again distinguish. Any act for the benefit of our own offspring may be useful, wise, and prudent, and, if well conceived and carefully carried out, may be called good, in one sense. But not till we know the motive, should we call it good in the other sense. In a primitive state of society children constituted the wealth and strength of a family, and to feed them and keep them from danger was no more meritorious than the feeding and keeping of slaves and cattle. From a purely utilitarian point of view, however, it would be useful, and therefore good, not to rear weak or crippled children, but to kill them, and here for the first time real goodness comes in. Real goodness is always, in some form or other, unselfishness. The unselfishness of a mother in bringing up a child that must always be a trouble and burden to her may be very misguided, anything but good in the eyes of those who interpret good as useful; but nevertheless, so long as the word *good* exists, it has always been applied to such acts.

In this case, however, the psychologist may still discover traces of selfishness in the natural love of a mother. But in the third sphere of action, in our endeavor to preserve and prolong the life of our fellow creatures, or, more correctly, in our endeavors to promote their general happiness, we can easily distinguish between acts that ought to be called good, simply in the sense of useful, and acts that ought to be called good, in the sense of unselfish. A man who fulfils the general duties necessary for keeping a community together may be called a good, that is, a useful citizen. He is useful to society, but he is useful also to himself, as a member of that society. A man, however, who, like Marcus Curtius, jumped into the abyss in order to save Rome, may no doubt be called a fool by utilitarian philosophers, but the Romans called him good, and we too must call him unselfish. And a man who, like Gordon, remained at his post, trusting in his God and in his country, may be called a madman; but no one would dare to call him selfish, and posterity will keep for him a place of honor among the heroes, among the martyrs, among the good men of England.

Philosophers are perfectly justified in attempting to build up systems of ethics on utilitarian and hedonistic principles. We should not even contest their right to give a new definition of *goodness*, and to say that with them it shall mean nothing but *usefulness*. But they must not play with language, and tell us that what the world meant by *good* was never more than what they mean by *useful*. On the contrary, the word *good* was framed originally to signify acts which were not useful, nay, which might be detrimental to the agent, and which, nevertheless, require our approval. Their usefulness depends on the means which we employ, goodness on the objects which we have in view. We may call useful what is selfish, we can never call what is selfish good.

There is no sphere of mental activity which does not stand in need of the corrective influence of the Science of Thought. If soldiers must look to their swords, philosophers will have to look to their words. I know that here, as elsewhere, inquiry into the supply, and a vigorous test of the efficiency, of words will be declared a nuisance, will be resisted and resented as an insult. But, in spite of all that, it will come, in some departments of thought it has already come, and in the future battles of the world good swords and good words will carry the day.

INDEX.

The Religion of Science Library.

A collection of bi-monthly publications, most of which are reprints of books published by The Open Court Publishing Company. Yearly, $1.50. Separate copies according to prices quoted. The books are printed upon good paper, from large type.

The Religion of Science Library, by its extraordinarily reasonable price, will bring a large number of valuable books within the reach of all readers.

The following have already appeared in the series:

No. 1. *The Religion of Science.* By PAUL CARUS. 25c.
2. *Three Introductory Lectures on the Science of Thought.* By F. MAX MÜLLER. 25c.
3. *Three Lectures on the Science of Language.* By F. MAX MÜLLER. 25c.
4. *The Diseases of Personality.* By TH. RIBOT. 25c.
5. *The Psychology of Attention.* By TH. RIBOT. 25c.
6. *The Psychic Life of Micro-Organisms.* By ALFRED BINET. 25c.
7. *The Nature of the State.* By PAUL CARUS. 15c.
8. *On Double Consciousness.* By ALFRED BINET. 15c.
9. *Fundamental Problems.* By PAUL CARUS. 50c.
10. *The Diseases of the Will.* By TH. RIBOT. 25c.
11. *The Origin of Language.* By LUDWIG NOIRÉ. 15c.
12. *The Free Trade Struggle in England.* By M. M. TRUMBULL. 25c.
13. *Wheelbarrow on the Labor Question.* By M. M. TRUMBULL. 35c.
14. *The Gospel of Buddha.* By PAUL CARUS. 35c.
15. *The Primer of Philosophy.* By PAUL CARUS. 25c.

The following are in preparation:

The Philosophy of Ancient India. By PROF. RICHARD GARBE.
Buddhism and Christianity. By PAUL CARUS.
The Lost Manuscript. A Novel. By GUSTAV FREYTAG.
The Study of Sanskrit. By PROF. H. OLDENBERG.
Old Testament History. By PROF. C. H. CORNILL.
Memory as a General Function of Organised Matter, and *The Specific Energies of the Nervous System*, etc. By PROF. EWALD HERING.

THE OPEN COURT PUBLISHING CO.,

324 DEARBORN STREET, CHICAGO, ILL.

CATALOGUE OF PUBLICATIONS

OF THE

OPEN COURT PUBLISHING CO.

MÜLLER, F. MAX.

THREE INTRODUCTORY LECTURES ON THE SCIENCE OF THOUGHT.

With a correspondence on "Thought Without Words," between F. Max Müller and Francis Galton, the Duke of Argyll, George J. Romanes and others. 128 pages. Cloth, 75 cents. Paper, 25 cents.

THREE LECTURES ON THE SCIENCE OF LANGUAGE.

The Oxford University Extension Lectures, with a Supplement, "My Predecessors," an essay on the genesis of "The Science of Thought.' 112 pages. Second Edition. Cloth, 75 cents. Paper, 25 cents.

ROMANES, GEORGE JOHN.

DARWIN AND AFTER DARWIN.

An Exposition of the Darwinian Theory and a Discussion of Post-Darwinian Questions.

1. THE DARWINIAN THEORY.
   460 pages. 125 illustrations. Cloth, $2.00.

2. POST-DARWINIAN QUESTIONS.
   Edited by Prof. C. Lloyd Morgan. Pages, 338. Cloth, $1.50. Both volumes, on one order, for $3.00 net.

AN EXAMINATION OF WEISMANNISM.

236 pages. Cloth, $1.00.

THOUGHTS ON RELIGION.

Edited by Charles Gore, M. A., Canon of Westminster. Second Edition. Pages, 184. Cloth, gilt top, $1.25.

COPE, E. D.

THE PRIMARY FACTORS OF ORGANIC EVOLUTION.

121 cuts. *Circa* 550 pages. Cloth, $2.00.

RIBOT, TH.

THE PSYCHOLOGY OF ATTENTION.

Authorised translation, 121 pages. Cloth, 75 cents. Paper, 25 cents.

THE DISEASES OF PERSONALITY.

Authorised translation, 157 pages. Cloth, 75 cents. Paper, 25 cents.

THE DISEASES OF THE WILL.

Authorised translation, 134 pages. Cloth, 75 cents. Paper, 25 cents.

N. B. Full set, cloth, net, $1.75.

MACH, ERNST.

THE SCIENCE OF MECHANICS.

A CRITICAL AND HISTORICAL EXPOSITION OF ITS PRINCIPLES. Translated from the second German edition by THOMAS J. MCCORMACK, with 250 cuts and illustrations, marginal analysis, and a complete index. 518 pages. Half morocco, gilt top. Price, $2.50.

POPULAR SCIENTIFIC LECTURES.

313 pages. Cloth, gilt top. Net, $1.00.

THE ANALYSIS OF THE SENSATIONS.

(In preparation.)

FREYTAG, GUSTAV.

THE LOST MANUSCRIPT.

A Novel. Authorised translation from the Sixteenth German Edition Two volumes. 953 pages. Extra cloth, gilt top, $4.00; the same in one volume, cloth, $1.00; paper, 75 cents.